Newnes
MS-DOS
Pocket Book

Newnes
MS-DOS
Pocket Book

Ian Sinclair

Heinemann Newnes

Heinemann Newnes
An imprint of Heinemann Professional Publishing Ltd
Halley Court, Jordan Hill, Oxford OX2 8EJ

OXFORD LONDON MELBOURNE AUCKLAND SINGAPORE
IBADAN NAIROBI GABORONE KINGSTON

First published 1989
Reprinted 1989

British Library Cataloguing in Publication Data

Sinclair, Ian
  Newnes MS-DOS pocket book.
  1. Microcomputer systems. Operating systems.
  MS-DOS & PC-DOS
  I. Title
  005.4'46

ISBN 0 434 91858 X

Typeset by Electronic Village Ltd, Richmond
Printed in England by Clays Ltd, St Ives plc

Contents

Preface

The aim of this book is to provide in easily portable
form a useful and comprehensive guide to the MS-
DOS operating system for computers of the PC class
(using the 8088, 8086 80286 or 80386 chips). It would
be possible to reduce the essentials of MS-DOS to a
few lines for each command, but the aim here has
been to provide rather more, enough information to
ensure that you can be confident in your use of a
command even if you have never used that command
previously, though not as much as would be provided
in an exhaustive text, nor as much as would be
required by an assembly-language programmer using
MS-DOS routines.

In addition, some background on the origins of
MS-DOS has been included, because, to use the
famous phrase, it's easier to tell where you are going
if you know where you have been. The bulk of this
book concerns the *user* of DOS, assisting with the
day to day control of the loading of programs and
data, backing up files, checking files and disks and
the integrity of data. To this has been added some
information on the inside working of DOS for the
user who may need to create short programs in
assembly language or in higher level languages
(Pascal, C or even BASIC) and needs to know how
these languages interact with MS-DOS.

The book is not concerned only with the
commands of DOS, but with how the computer is set
up, using the AUTOEXEC.BAT file and the
CONFIG.SYS file, since these important parts of the
set-up are often omitted in books that cover MS-
DOS. The emphasis is on the use of the machine with
a hard disk, but users of single/double floppy
machines will also find much that is applicable. The
aim is to provide a reference guide for the user that
will be *used* and carried around rather than gathering
dust on a shelf.

I am most grateful to Peter Dixon of Heinemann
Professional Publishing for suggesting this title, and
to Microsoft Inc. for the information that they
supply to computer manufacturers. I also wish to
acknowledge the contribution of PDSL (see
Appendix D) in providing utility software and much
useful information.

Ian Sinclair

1 The beginnings

When micro-computers started to be used seriously
for business purposes, many manufacturers devised
their own operating systems. The operating system is
a program that either exists in the computer in the
form of a chip (a ROM system) or can be loaded in
from a disk, using a very small loader system in
ROM. The aim of the operating system is to provide,
at the very least, the essential routines that allow the
computer to make use of the screen, the keyboard
and the disk drive(s), managing files and loading and
running programs. Without program routines that
attend to these tasks, the computer is unusable, so
that the operating system is just as important as all
the hardware of the computer.

The use of different operating systems by different
manufacturers, however, makes it virtually impossible
to set standards that will allow one computer to run
a program that works on another computer from a
different manufacturer. When all computers were
mainframes, with one computer to one company,
with programs specially written for the machine,
interchangeability of programs was of no importance.
The prospect that each user of a computer might
eventually be working with a separate machine came
only with the development of microcomputers, and
only when corporate users started to take microcomputers seriously. To see what the attitude of corporate
users was to microcomputers, it is interesting to look
at some of the textbooks of Computer Science which
are still used in schools, some of which seem almost
intended to discourage computing as a career.

One solution to the problem of interchangeability
came about in the very early days of the development
of microcomputers, in the form of CP/M. This was
a system to control, program and monitor (hence the
initials) the operation of these early microcomputers,
and it was devised by Gary Kildall in or around 1973,
before microcomputers were a commercial proposi-
tion. At that time, the idea of an operating system
was not new because Unix was already under
development for mainframe machines, but the idea
of a standard operating system for microcomputers
was certainly new.

The Intel 8080 microprocessor, around which many
early microcomputers for business use was designed,
first appeared in 1975, and CP/M was quickly

adapted to it. Though some of the machines which made most of the running in these early days, such as Apple-2, Commodore PET and Tandy TRS-80, used their own operating systems, the advantages of a standard system was recognised by many other manufacturers who were able to market machines for business use which could interchange programs and data provided that their disk formats were compatible. Unfortunately, no standard for disk formats existed at that time, so that the advantages of using CP/M were often diminished by the inability to exchange disks directly, though programs and data could be exchanged by way of the serial ports (which were, of course, controlled by CP/M), and by programs which could be used to allow a machine to read a disk that had been formatted in a different way.

One particularly valuable feature of CP/M was that it came along with a set of utility programs that allowed the user to carry out tasks like file copying, file checking, program modification, disk verification and all of the other housekeeping actions that are now so familiar. Some of these programs had been devised in the very early days of micro-computer use, and were intended for the programmer rather than the user.

In these days, however, microcomputers were bought in the main by people who understood computer programing, or who were determined to learn, so that these utilities were welcomed even though their use was by no means easy. The idea of a program being user-friendly was a few years away, as was the idea of really widespread use of computers.

The IBM PC

The start of serious small-scale computing as we know it today was with the IBM PC machine, which was released in 1981. The original PC machine was designed around a new microprocessor chip, the Intel 8088, which allowed data to be handled internally in 16-bit form rather than the 8-bit form that had been standard in the CP/M machines which used the 8080 or Z-80 chips. Data was, however, read and written in 8-bit form, in contrast to the companion Intel chip the 8086. The 8088 was chosen for the IBM PC because at the time the 8086 chip was difficult to mass-produce, but later PC-compatible machines have taken advantage of falling chip prices to use the superior 8086 rather than the older 8088.

Both of these chips, however, have a structure which was very much a development of the older 8080 chip (also by Intel), so that it was possible to revise programs that had worked on the earlier CP/M machines so as to run on the new IBM PC. Before the machine could be released, however, it needed an operating system, one that would provide the facilities of CP/M on an extended scale for a complete new generation of 16-bit machines.

Digital Research, the company that had been set up to market and develop CP/M, offered a new version, CP/M-86, which could be used on the PC type of machine. At the same time, however, the rival software house Microsoft were using a 16-bit operating system which had been developed by a smaller firm, Seattle Computer Products in 1980, and which at one time was termed QDOS, with the QD meaning Quick and Dirty. This was renamed 86-DOS and with intensive effort was developed into a powerful operating system which was offered to IBM at a price that considerably undercut CP/M-86.

The system as used on the PC was known as PC-DOS, and a virtually identical version was available for any other manufacturers of machines using the Intel chips, using the name MS-DOS. This has progressed through many versions (now version 4.0) as the demands for new facilities has expanded; the main changes in the later versions have been to allow for networking use and for use with the 80386 type of machine in which the memory limitations of earlier versions are overcome.

Chip Development

The first IBM PC machine used only 16K of RAM, and in its standard form used cassette tape rather than disks. Disk drives could be added, however, with a memory extension to 64K, which seemed adequate at the time, since all of the standard business programs (such as WordStar, SuperCalc, dBase-2) ran under CP/M in this amount of memory space on the CP/M machines and could be converted to run in the same amount of space on the new machine. The 8088 chip and its stable-mate the 8086 allowed up to 1 Mbyte of memory to be used, however, so that pressure soon built up for the use of more memory.

The Intel chips have always been designed to offer a complete set of computing actions along with quite exceptional compatibility, and the history of MS-DOs closely parallels the work that has been done in the development of these chips. Though there are versions of MS-DOS that run as 'simulations' on machines with a different chip set, the use of MS-DOs has always been aimed at the Intel chips. This, in particular, affects the way that memory can be extended and used.

In particular, decisions that were taken a long time ago still affect what is easily possible. When the Intel 8088/8086 chips were being designed in 1979 the price and performance of RAM was such that no-one envisaged more than 1 M-byte of total memory ever being used, and the simplest way of retaining the compatibility between the new chips and the old was to manage memory in 64 K pieces, each piece being called a *segment*. This allowed several important advantages, not least of which was that the new chips could use many of the design features of the old ones.

One important point was that the registers that controlled the use of a segment of memory could be identical to the registers that were used in the 8-bit chips, and the choice of different segments could be achieved by placing a segment number into another register. This, in turn, allowed for the possibility of using programs that would run in a 64K segment, with a different program in each segment, or as an alternative, the use of programs which would take up more than one segment, like the bloated monsters of 360K and more that we are familiar with today.

MS-DOS Development

As the demand for the PC grew, and the disk system was standardised to the familiar 5.25″ 40-track double-sided double-density format, MS-DOS was being steadily developed to cope with new needs. One restriction that has remained on MS-DOS is one of memory management. MS-DOS was originally written to cater for a maximum of ten segments of RAM, corresponding to 640K, and this has to date never changed, though version 4.0 allows for the use of both extended and expanded memory (see later for explanation). The limit is fixed by the use of a 1Mb address limit on the original 8088/8086 chips, which both use a 20-line address bus, so that the address range covers 2^{20} addresses. This is 1,048,576, which is one megabyte (1Mb.), allowing 640K for RAM and the remaining 384K for ROM and for RAM that is used for the screen display.

The development of higher-resolution screen displays from the original text only, through monochrome graphics to colour graphics of the CGA, VGA and EGA variety, has made increasing inroads into the memory allowance, and a further piece has been taken by the hard-disk ROM (whether the hard disk is built in or added as a card). The later 80286 chip was constructed in a way that allowed it to handle up to 16 Mb of memory – but only when running a different operating system such as Xenix or Unix, and it retained the 1 Mb limit for MS-DOS. Only the 80386 chip, of those announced and being delivered to date, overcomes the problems of 64K segments and the 1 Mb memory limit – but MS-DOS has not adapted fully to this freedom.

It is true that the latest version. MS-DOS 4.0 has provision for using add-on memory, the type called *expanded* memory which is added in the form of a card, and switched into circuit as required. This should not be confused with *extended* memory which can be added to 80286 and 80386 machines. These machines use a 24-line address bus so that 16 Mb can be addressed, and memory that is installed beyond the original 1 Mb limit on such machine is extended memory, which can be used only by programs that have been written to do so.

Neither form of added memory can be used, at present, in any simple way. MS-DOS therefore does not provide for multi-tasking, meaning that two or more programs can be run in the memory at the same time, when this 640K requirement is exceeded. The MS Windows system allows for more than one program to be present, and for switching easily between programs, but all within the 640K limit, using a hard disk to store a program and data while the use of the program is suspended.

Windows allows for true multi-tasking only on the 80386 type of machine (using Windows-386), and the 640K barrier is broken by the later operating system, OS-2 rather than by MS-DOS. However, OS-2 requires very much more memory for its own purposes, and is intended for machines with many Mb of RAM memory, and it is possible that later versions of MS-DOS, beyond 4.1, may offer multi-tasking without being so demanding on memory.

DOS Versions

The original versions of MS-DOS were 1.0 and 1.1. These were suited to the older version of the PC, and V.1.0 could be used only with single-sided disk drives. V.1.1, which allowed the use of the familiar double-sided disk, was released in 1982. These early versions were rare in Europe, where the PC type of machine was not outstandingly popular at first.

Versions 2.0 and 2.1 were written to expand the use of MS-DOS very considerably when the PC was almost universally supplied with a disk system and more memory, often with 360K or more. At this time, clones of the PC began to appear, some of which provided as standard many of the facilities that had been available on the original machine only by way of plug-in cards. The most important of the additions that were made to MS-DOS at that time were to cope with TSR programs, country-variables, hard disk use, and file handling.

A Terminate-and-stay-resident program (TSR) is one that can be loaded into a segment and which will then stay in that segment, being activated and deactivated as needed within a computing session without the need to be re-loaded. The use of such programs involves the allocation of memory and the protection of that memory in order to make sure that no other program is loaded over the TSR program.

There also must be provision for 'hot-key' use, so that a key combination, such as Alt-Shift can start or stop the TRS program. What is *not* usually provided for is the removal of a TSR program cleanly from the memory so that the memory can be released for other use. This often means that loading in a large program, such as a desk-top publishing package or a large program like Lotus Agenda or Symphony can lead to Out of memory messages, and the program can be run successfully only if the machine is re-booted first. There are utilities for freeing memory, but they do not appear to be widely available.

Country variables refer to the keyboard and screen characters that will appear in versions of MS-DOS that run on machines which are used with a character set other than the standard US one. This is provided for in DOS versions from 2.0 on, but versions 2.0 and 2.1 provide only for getting this information, not for easily changing it. The ability to view and modify the country variables was completely implemented in version 3.0.

The provision for hard disk drives was a particularly important step forward. This was made necessary because of the fast rate of development of miniature hard disks from the 8″ size to 5.25″ and then to 3.5″, making it possible to have a hard disk in the space of a floppy drive, or even on a card that would fit into one of the slots inside the computer. The familiar commands that were added at this time include MKDIR (or MD) to make a disk directory, CHDIR (or CD) to switch to a named directory, and RMDIR (or RD) to remove a directory. The drive memory limit was set at 32 Mb, after which the disk drive had to be *partitioned* as if it were more than one drive. At the same time, MS-DOS 2.0 added a large number of routines for handling files, most of which are not accessible directly through command names but which can be used by programmers working in assembly language or in some higher level languages, notably C. The EXIT command was also added, which makes it possible to jump out of a program (the *parent* program) to use DOS (as a *child* program), and then (by typing EXIT and then pressing the RETURN key) to return to the program. Not all programs are written in order to take advantage of this.

Another major addition was a supplementary way of controlling files. The earlier versions of MS-DOS had used the same method of keeping track of files as CP/M, a method called file control blocks (FCB). With MS-DOS 2.0, this older method was supplemented by a set of new routines which could use a much simpler method, a file handle. Without going into detail, using a file control block meant that a set of bytes in memory had to be used to hold, in correct order, all the details of a file, and this form of memory block had to be set up for each file. The file handle method allowed a simple string of ASCII characters, consisting of drive letter and full filename, to be used as a file control by assigning a 16-bit code number, with all the rest of the work performed by the operating system. The file-handle system also allowed peripherals like the printer and the serial port to be used as if they were files, with names such as PRN and AUX1. Programs could still be written using the older method, because it was still available on DOS 2.0 and beyond, but the file handle method is so much easier to use that most programmers have taken advantage of it.

There were also some useful minor additions in MS-DOS 2.0, such as the ability to control the use of the Break key, and the ability to rename a file and to label a file with date and time. Also added was the information on the space remaining on a disk (following the disk directory) and the VER command to get the MS-DOS version number.

The large changes between versions 1.1 and 2.0 or 2.1 meant that programs that were written to take full advantage of version 2.0 or 2.1 could not be used with 1.0 or 1.1. This incompatibility was less serious that it seemed, because the major changes that had taken place in the requirements for DOS, such as hard disk use, made it pointless to write programs that would use the older version, and it was still possible to run programs that had run under the older versions. The changes that were made from version 2.1 to version 3.0 (followed in quick succession by 3.1, 3.2, 3.3 and 3.4) were not so dramatic from the point of view of the user of a single machine, but they added significant extensions. The main extensions concerned the use of programs by computers that were part of a network. Networking requires changes to the operating system in order to make certain that one computer does not, without permission, alter the files that belong to another, and quite extensive additions to MS-DOS had to be made in order to satisfy the requirements. For users of solo machines, however, these had no impact, but the addition of pipes and filters did.

The principles of pipes and filters had existed for a considerable time in the Unix operating system for mainframe computers, but they had not previously been implemented in an operating system for a microcomputer. A pipe implies that a command symbol will allow data to be channelled from one program to another, or from a program to a different outlet (to printer, for example, rather than to screen). A filter means that a program which can modify data can be placed in the way of data that is being transferred. For example, data that is to be shown on the screen can have a filter inserted that will ensure that it appears in alphabetical order, or it can be arranged to appear 24 lines at a time so that the user has time to look at one screen before seeing the next 24 lines. Redirection of this type was the main step forward in version 3.0 as far as the single user was concerned.

As a more minor change, the country variables could now be set by the use of KEYB files, such as KEYBUK which sets the keyboard for the UK character set, with the pound sign, and with the single and double quote marks in positions that are transposed in comparison to the US keyboard. Version 3.2 also introduced support for 3.5" disk drives, allowing a change to this size of disk. This was rather belated as far as the PC was concerned, because machines such as the Apple Macintosh, Amiga and Atari ST had shown the advantages of the smaller and better-protected disks. In general, most users of MS-DOS should by this time be using version 3.0 at the earliest, and many will have obtained version 3.3 or 3.4 with their computers in recent years, though very few at the time of writing have V.4.0 or later. The differences between the various sub-versions since 3.0 are less important than the step from 2.2 to 3.0, and it is not advisable to run any modern program on version 2.1 or earlier.

Version 4.0

Version 4.0 became available in 1988, and seems to be intended as a way of preparing users for the use of OS/2 (which has been long delayed). The 32 Mb limit on the hard disk drive was removed, so that partitioning is no longer needed, and at last there was some use of memory above the 640K limit. The main difference for the user, however, is that the screen presentation has changed to the windows/icon/mouse style.

V.4.0 is contained as standard on two 3.5" disks since it will be supplied mainly with machines that use 3.5" disks, though if any manufacturer intended to use MS-DOS 4.0 on a machine that used 5.25 disks the program would be available on these disks. One disk is labelled as an Install disk, and is used to boot in the operating system in the usual way. Normally, DOS 4.0 will be supplied only with a new machine whose hard disk will be un-configured, but if you change to V.4.0 from an older version such as 3.3, then you can expect to run into trouble if your hard disk is already partitioned.

Another novelty is the automatic creation of CONFIG.SYS and AUTOEXEC.BAT files, along with a new file, DOSSHELL.BAT which controls other aspect of use, such as mouse support and the command display. This now provides the option of using Command Prompt, which means that programs can be run in the same way as on older versions, by typing the program name (and drive/directory-path if needed) or by using the File System which allows selection by mouse.

The amount of extra memory needed for these systems, however, means that some programs, notably large graphics programs like Lotus Freelance, will not have enough memory to run, even if expanded memory is present to be used by DOS. The original version of Microsoft Windows 386 will not work with DOS 4.0, though a later version 2.10 will do so. On the whole, since Microsoft are reluctant to release any details of V.4.0 other than to computer manufacturers, it is better to use DOS 4.0 on computers that come with the system than to attempt to upgrade on your present machine.

COM and EXE files

MS-DOS can run two types of machine-code program which use the extension filenames of COM and EXE respectively. A COM file is constructed almost identically to a CP/M file (which would also carry the COM extension), and the entire program, along with all of its data and other use of memory, is contained in a single 64K segment. MS-DOS will decide which segment is selected (always the lowest-numbered part of the available memory), and because all of the program is contained within a 64K address space the address numbers can use single-word (16-bit) registers. This makes it possible to design and use short and memory-efficient programs, and also to have several such programs present in memory at any given time.

The alternative is the EXE type of program which will usually make use of more than one segment. In addition, such a program can be relocated anywhere in the memory (subject to rules about where it would start in a given segment) and will still run. This is the method that must be followed for larger programs, or programs in which data needs a separate segment. When an EXE program is loaded, MS-DOS will place it wherever it can be put. The organisation of memory in the PC type of machine is illustrated here

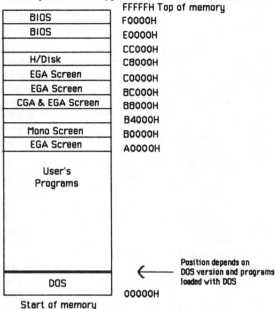

Figure 1.1 Organization of memory in the PC using MS-DOS

with addresses up to 1Mb in hex (00000H to FFFFFH). On the 8088/8086 machines, this upper memory limit is determined by the number of address lines, but on the 80286 and 80386 machines the limit is determined by MS-DOS itself. The forthcoming 80486 chip machines are unlikely to make use of MS-DOS, and will probably be used with OS2 or a variant or Unix.

The normal amount of RAM memory is therefore in the 640K range, and of this DOS takes an amount which is typically 70K for versions prior to 4.0. As well as the amount taken up by DOS, it is likely that your AUTOEXEC.BAT file will see to the loading of various other programs, such as GRAPHICS, all of which take up more memory space. It is possible, then, to find that the lowest memory address that is free is around 140K above the start of the memory.

2 The MS-DOS main files

MS-DOS relies on several files to achieve its effects. One of these files is normally held in a ROM chip, and is known as the BIOS, Basic Input-Output System. This part of the operating system is provided by the manufacturer of the computer, who is therefore responsible for its contents and its correct interaction with the rest of the system. For the IBM PC and several of its clones, the ROM BIOS is the IBM version. Other manufacturers, such as Amstrad, will have their own names and copyright information coded into the ROM BIOS, but there are a few examples in circulation of machines whose makers deny any connection with IBM but whose BIOS chips carry the IBM copyright notice.

Irrespective of its design, the BIOS in ROM must carry out the elementary input and output actions, and it must do so using certain fixed starting addresses that will be used by MS-DOS. Any manufacturer can therefore design a BIOS chip, and a licence from IBM is necessary only if that particular chip is duplicated, or so closely copied as to make it a duplicate in all but name. Some early copies were detected because they copied the known errors in the BIOS chip as well as all of the standard routines. The BIOS address area is at the top of the memory, and a lot more space is reserved than is normally needed, so allowing for additional BIOS ROMs to be used. For example, the Amstrad version of BIOS, called ROS (Resident Operating System) occupies only 16K of the 64K which is reserved for BIOS use. There is an additional 192K allocation of memory lying under the BIOS region which is also reserved for expansion ROMs, and when a hard disk drive is fitted, the ROM that is on the hard-disk driver card will use some 16K of this space, leaving plenty of room for another hard disk unit to be used. In some computers, you will find more than one copy of the BIOS in the reserved addresses.

The system files

The rest of the work is done by files that are read in from the disk, and one of the tasks of the BIOS in ROM is to allow the other files to be read, put them into the correct places in the memory (at the lowest end of the memory) and to start them running. The names of these files depend on the software that has been supplied with the machine. On the IBM machine, these files are called IBMBIO.SYS and IBMDOS.SYS, but on most other machines they will have other names, typically IO.SYS and MSDOS.SYS. The first of these is an addition to the input/output facilities of the BIOS in ROM, and the second is used to carry out some of the MS-DOS (or PC-DOS) actions. These files should be the first two files stored on the disk, and if they are not found the system will halt and issue the error message:

```
Non-System disk or disk error
Replace and strike any key when ready
```

The floppy drive A is *always* checked first for these files, and even if you always start the machine from a hard disk, you will get this error message and then a hang-up if there is a disk without system tracks in drive A. The remedy if you use a hard disk is always to start the machine with drive A empty.

If the system tracks are found, the IO.SYS and MSDOS.SYS files are read and placed at the lowest end of the memory. The IO.SYS program starts to run, and calls the MSDOS.SYS program. It is during this time that the memory of the machine is checked. When the IO.SYS program starts running again, it will configure the machine according to the lines in the CONFIG.SYS file (see Chapter 6). In addition, there is a file called COMMAND.COM, which is used for most of the built-in commands of MS-DOS, the actions which are carried out when a word is typed and the RETURN/ENTER key pressed. The COMMAND.COM file is loaded by a routine in MS-DOS, and it is arranged so that part of it is retained in the memory so that essential actions (the internal commands) are available when needed, but the other part of COMMAND.COM can be (and often is) wiped out by parts of other programs. This is because this *transient* part of COMMAND.COM is loaded into the top end of memory, and since MS-DOS will allocate the whole of the memory to a program unless instructed otherwise, it is quite usual for this part of COMMAND.COM to be replaced. When this has happened, users of floppy disk machines will get a message:

```
Insert disk with COMMAND.COM into Drive A
```

so that the missing part of the file can be restored.

Users of a hard disk that has been correctly set up with a path (see later) to COMMAND.COM will never see this message, because the re-loading is automatic.

Of all the files that make up MS-DOS, COMMAND.COM is the most visible in the sense that it appears in the disk directory and is the subject of the message when floppy disks are being used. The other two files in RAM are *hidden* files, meaning that they do not appear in a conventional listing using the DIR command. This is done deliberately, along with making the files read-only and delete-protected, to prevent you from working on these files, perhaps deleting them accidentally with a command that would wipe all of the files from the disk. The presence of these files, along with COMMAND.COM, makes the difference between a *system* floppy disk and a *data* floppy disk. For example, using MS-DOS 3.2, on a disk that has been formatted for data 362,496 bytes are free for use, but on a system disk you will find only 291,840 free. The difference of 70656 is due to the various MS-DOS files. The precise size of the various files changes in each new issue of MS-DOS, so that these figures are for one version only.

COMMAND.COM

The COMMAND.COM file is used along with the hidden files to implement MS-DOS, and it is important to ensure that you use the correct version of COMMAND.COM. As various versions of MS-DOS have appeared, COMMAND.COM has changed also, so that if you use a COMMAND.COM from MS-DOS V. 3.3 along with the hidden files from MS-DOS V. 3.2, then at some stage you will get an error message to the effect that COMMAND.COM is not present, or that the wrong version is present. Use of the wrong version is particularly easy if you use a hard-disk system with COMMAND.COM in the root directory. If you then carelessly copy a floppy disk which is a system disk, the COMMAND.COM file from that disk will replace the COMMAND.COM on the hard disk, and you will from then on use the new COMMAND.COM. No harm will come of this if the new COMMAND.COM is identical to the old value, but if it is not, then there will inevitably be problems.

COMMAND.COM also figures in the fashionable

scare of 1988, the virus infection. Since it is so easy to install COMMAND.COM into a hard disk, either from a floppy or by way of files received over a telephone contact, a doctored version can be substituted. These doctored versions can contain extra pieces of code which can be activated by a date (like Friday 13th in any month) or by the use of one particular command, and their effect can range from the comical but annoying to the downright destructive. The problem should not be overstated – it affects (that is, if it exists at all) computers which are left unattended and connected to telephone lines with their main files unprotected. There are also a few viruses that are passed by way of disks that purport to contain utilities or games, so that disk-swapping at conferences is now hazardous (as well as everything else). If your computer is not on a network, you do not leave it on-line so that anyone can make contact and you do not accept free disks from dubious sources, the possibility of a virus infection is very remote. If, in addition, you use floppy disks rather than a hard disk system, then a virus would be little more than a temporary nuisance.

One useful precaution that you can take to defend your COMMAND.COM file is to note its length. When you use the DIR command to print a disk directory, the length of each file is shown, and you should note the length of each version of COMMAND.COM that you have, either on floppy or on hard disk. Somewhere, safely locked away in cool dry place, you will have the original system disks that came with the computer, or were bought as an update for MS-DOS. Find the file length number for the version of COMMAND.COM that is on the MS-DOS system disk for this set. This ought to be the definitive version for your computer, and any version of COMMAND.COM that is longer than this one should be suspect as either a later version (which will not match the other files) or an infected version. It is also possible to make COMMAND.COM a read-only file. MS-DOS permits four *attributes* (out of a possible eight) to be altered for each and every disk file. These are *Archive*, *Read-only*, *Hidden*, and *System*. The methods of altering these in MS-DOS are rather crude, and many programs that you can buy to make the use of DOS easier allow simpler methods of checking and altering the attributes. The Archive attribute is used to determine which files are to be backed up when a backup utility is used, and this is of importance mainly to the user of a hard disk, since it can be employed to ensure that only files which have been altered since a previous backup are marked as due for a backup. The Read-only attribute allows the file to appear in the directory, but for reading only; any attempt to write to this file or erase it will be met with an error message. The Hidden attribute makes the file disappear from the directory, and the System attribute is used similarly to hide and protect system files, the MSDOS.SYS and IO.SYS types of files, which usually have System, Hidden and Read-only attributes set.

By setting the Read-only attribute for COMMAND.COM, you can prevent this file being altered or deleted, but this can be rather a mixed blessing. If your computer is one of the modern PC clone variety, such as the Amstrad, then it will have a clock system which keeps running on battery power when the computer is switched off. This replaces the infuriating old system in which you have to enter the time and data each time you switch on the computer. If, however, you make COMMAND.COM into a Read-only file, then you will be forced to enter time and date just as you do on the older machines (though if you don't need to have time and date in programs you can, of course, simply ignore this). The clock circuits that are used on the later machines need to be able to pass their data into COMMAND.COM in order to connect with the DATE and TIME commands of COMMAND.COM, and if COMMAND.COM is Read-only, then this information cannot be passed on.

Filenames

Whichever version of DOS you use will require you to specify names for your files, and MS-DOS follows, as far as floppy-disk users are concerned, the same requirements as CP/M. In addition, any programs that make use of the DOS (and practically all do) will impose the same rules on filenames, so you need to be familiar with what is required. To start with, there are names that you cannot and must not use. You cannot use any of the names that appear on the Master Disc, because these are reserved for the programs that bear these names.

In addition, there are 'internal' commands, stored

in the memory, whose names you must not use. These are:

BREAK	CD	CHCP	CHDIR	CLS
COPY	CTTY	DATE	DEL	DIR
ECHO	ERASE	EXIT	FILES	FOR
GOTO	IF	MKDIR	MD	PATH
PAUSE	PROMPT	RENAME	REM	RMDIR
RD	SET	SHIFT	TIME	TYPE
VER	VERIFY	VOL		

Any attempt to use these names other than for the programs that they represent will cause problems. If you work with the MS-DOS distribution disk in place, or with a path (hard disk users) to the MS-DOS external command programs, then you need to avoid using any of these filenames also. These are:

APPEND	ASSIGN	ATTRIB	BACKUP
CHKDSK	COMMAND	COMP	COUNTRY
DISKCOMP	DISKCOPY	EXE2BIN	FASTOPEN
FDISK	FIND	FORMAT	GRAFTABL
GRAPHICS	JOIN	KEYB	KEYBUK
LABEL	MODE	MORE	NLSFUNC
PRINT	RECOVER	REPLACE	RESTORE
SELECT	SHARE	SORT	SUBST
SYS	TREE	XCOPY	

Various programs that you use will also have their own prohibitions, all designed to prevent you from damaging essential files on the disks. In general, a suitable filename will consist of up to eight characters, the first of which must be a letter. The other characters can be letters, or you can use the digits 0 to 9, or the symbols

$ # & @ ! % ( ) - _ { } / ` ^ '

The following characters *must not* be used:

* + = [ ] ; : , . / ?

nor can you use:

the space
the tab
the Ctrl character

Unless it's particularly important to you to use the permitted symbols, they are best avoided, particularly symbols like the single inverted quotes, which are easily confused or overlooked. A good rule is to use words with a digit or pair of digits used at the end to express versions, like TEXT1, TEXT2...TEXT15 and so on. Allowing up to eight characters means that you may have to abbreviate names that you would want to use, like ACCREC1 or BOTLEDG1, but it should be possible to provide a name that conveys to you what the file is all about. Whether you use lower-case or upper-case characters, MS-DOS will convert all filenames to upper-case.

Drive letter

The eight-character (or less) main name is essential, but there are two other parts to a filename that are optional. One of these is the drive letter. The PC type of machine labels its main drives as A (the only *physical* drive in a single-drive machine), B (second drive in a twin-floppy machine) and C. The C-drive on a machine that uses only floppy disk(s) can be a RAM-drive. On a machine that uses a hard disk, the C-drive is normally the hard disk, and the letter D will be used for a RAM-drive or for a second hard disk.

RAM-drive simply means that part of the memory is set aside and used like a disk, so that disk commands will store data to this memory or read data from it. This is useful for storing files that programs often make use of, like the dictionary of a spelling-checker. MS-DOS contains methods of setting aside memory for a RAM-DRIVE, and a particularly useful provision is for expanded memory (memory which is added on a plug-in board, and which can be switched in and out by software) to be used in this way. If you have only a single floppy drive and no hard disk, then you can ignore a lot of the information about drive letters, because only the A drive will physically be used; and possibly the letter C for RAM-drive. There is an important distinction, however, between a *physical* drive, meaning one that is physically present, and a logical drive. MS-DOS will, on a single floppy machine, assign the logical drive letters A and B for the single floppy drive. This allows you to call up programs such as:

```
B:callit
```

and get the message:

`Insert the disk for Drive B: in the drive`

so that you can make use of a single-drive system as if two drives were present

For the user of twin floppies, specifying a filename such as B:PROG, means that you are stipulating that the file will make use of the disk in drive B. The drive letter precedes the main part of the filename, and is separated from it (very important) with a colon. If no drive letter is used, of course, the colon is not needed. The machine will then use the default drive, whatever drive was last in use, or the A: drive if you have just switched a floppy-drive machine on. This use of a drive letter applies whether you want to load the program from the disk or record (save) it on to the disk. Similarly, using C:PROG will specify the use of the C drive, the RAM-drive or hard disk. Using a drive letter in a filename in this way specifies the drive only for the duration of the command that is used with the filename. In other words, if you have specified that you want to run a program B:TESTIT, then the program is loaded from drive B, but whenever the program has been loaded, the normal drive will be the one that was in use previously. This normally means that the program loads from drive B, and from then on, any use of disks will make use of the A drive again. If no change is made (using the command B:, for example) then the normal default drive is the A drive. MS-DOS has a set of commands that are particularly aimed at the hard disk user. These are dealt with later in this chapter.

Extension

As well as the drive letter, which is always a single letter placed ahead of the filename and separated by a colon, the complete filename can contain an 'extension'. The extension is a set of up to three letters that are added to the end of the filename, separated by a dot. Any letters following three will be ignored when the filename is typed. Like the disk drive letter, the extension is optional, and if it is not used, then the dot is not needed. The purpose of the extension is to convey some extra information about the type of file, though you can make whatever use of it suits your own purposes, within limits. Just as there are forbidden filenames, there are also forbidden extensions, and in particular you should not make use of the extensions .EXE, .BAK, .HEX, .COM or .OBJ for your files, because these are extensions that are used with special meanings. The list following shows a few 'standard' extension letters and their uses, and you should, if you use extensions at all, either keep to some of these or use some entirely different codes of your own.

BAK	A back-up file
BAS	A program that cannot be run unless BASIC has been loaded first.
BAT	A batch file of commands to the DOS.
COM	A program that can be loaded and run by typing its (main) name.
DOC	A text file of documentation for a program.
EXE	As for COM, but a longer program.
MSG	A text file of instructions.
SYS	A file that is used by the operating system.
TMP	A file that is created temporarily and wiped later.
$$$	Also a temporary file.

Particularly useful extensions for you to use are .TXT for files of text, as from a word processor, and .DAT for files of data as might be used in accounts programs. You will find that many programs that you will use will generate their own extensions for data that they save to disk, and you should not use these extensions for other files. It's particularly important to know at this point that any file with the extension of .BAK is a file that has been replaced with a more recent version with the same main filename. Some programs will not allow you to save a file with the same name as one that already exists on the disk. Others will automatically rename the existing file as a BAK file, and save your new file with a different extension. Many programs, however, will delete an old file that has the same name as one you are saving.

Wildcards in filenames

The term 'wildcard' sounds very fanciful when applied to computing, but it's a useful feature of most disk operating systems. The wildcard is a character, usually ? which can be used as a substitute for a character or * for a group of characters. When you use the asterisk wildcard you are saying, in effect, that you don't care what that part of a name is. For example, if you type

```
DIR *.COM
```

and press ENTER, you will get a listing of any files that have the extension letters of COM, whatever the main part of the filename happens to be. If you type:

```
DIR MA*.TXT
```

then (if the disk contains them) you will get names such as MAINONE.TXT, MANALIVE.TXT, MARTIN.TXT, MALLARD.TXT and so on. The ? wildcard is more selective, because it allows the substitution of one character only, so that using WORK?.TXT would allow files WORK0.TXT, WORK1.TXT, and so on up to WORK9.TXT to be used, but not WORK10.TXT or higher numbers.

The use of wildcards can be very convenient, allowing a lot of actions to be carried out with just one command. It can also be very inconvenient, causing you to delete a file accidentally just because you were deleting a group that happened to have similar names, for example. The asterisk is the wildcard that is most often used, because it's so convenient to be able to substitute for any number of characters. Not all commands allow the use of wildcards, and in some cases the use of wildcards can have unexpected results, so that in the following chapters, the use of a wildcardwith an instruction is noted along with the effects.

Hard disk sub-directories

Unlike a floppy disk, which has a capacity that can range from 360K for a 5.25″ DSDD floppy to 1.4 Mb for a 3.5″ high-density disk, the hard disk can contain a huge number of files which would require several pages of printout to list. Finding a file would therefore be extremely difficult unless some method were used of grouping files into sets. The method that is used is that of sub-directories.

A sub-directory is a file which is placed on the disk like any other file, but used to store other files and information on other files in the same form as would be used on a separate disk. This type of sub-directory file can be treated as if it were a disk of (almost) unlimited size, so that all of the files that are stored on a hard disk can be grouped into several of these sub-directories. By subdividing the directory, files can be kept in groups and you can call for a directory of one group only, greatly reducing the effort that you need to spend on finding anything useful. The scheme can be operated just as easily with floppy disks, but it is less necessary, because the storage capacity of a floppy disk is so much less than that of a hard disk. It's easier to use a separate floppy disk or group of floppy disks for a set of related files than to work with directory trees, though you will find directory trees used on floppy disks, since they are a useful way of protecting files from being erased by mistake. The use of sub-directories on floppy disks can also be a way of backing up a pattern of files on a hard disk, preserving the structure that the files have on the hard disk.

Directory trees

One way of thinking about this method of grouping files is to regard the main set of files on the disk as the *root* set, and the others as branches. This latter name is not well-chosen, because what is meant is smaller parts of roots, and the diagram that everyone shows you:

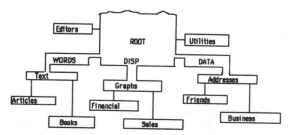

Figure 2.1 Tree diagram for directories and files

looks more like the roots of a tree than its branches. An alternative way of thinking about it is as a family tree, which starts with one ancestor and spreads out to all of the descendants. However you like to imagine it, the diagram indicates that when you call for a directory display, all that you will get initially is the set of names that appear in the first line, called the *root names*. In the example, these filenames are WORDS, DISP and DATA, names that are chosen to indicate what type of files will occupy the three sub-directories. Note that these names are not names of files but names of *other directories*. I have picked these names as illustrations only, because they show particularly well why it is useful to subdivide a directory in this way.

Ironically enough, it isn't always possible to put some programs into a sub-directory and use them effectively. Some of the older word-processing and spreadsheet programs must be placed in the root directory along with their data files if you want to be able to use them directly. This is an important point if you have just bought a hard disk machine and want to add software, and it's equally important if you are buying software for a floppy-disk machine that you later intend to upgrade to hard disk operation. Only programs that can run under the MS-DOS sub-directory structure should be bought unless you have an overwhelming need to use a program regardless of its flaws in this respect. If you make use of only one type of program on your hard disk, then it hardly matters that you are confined to the root directory.

Paths in filenames

The use of files in sub-directories makes the use of conventional filenames unsuitable. MS-DOS copes with this by allowing *paths* to be specified. A path is a set of sub-directory names which will end in the position of the file that you want. The sections of a filename that includes a path are separated by the backslash (\), and when a backslash is used as the first symbol in a path, this is taken to mean that the path starts in the root directory; otherwise the path starts at the current directory. The direction of a path must *always* be towards the more remote branches, never back towards the root. Suppose, for example, that you are using the root directory and want to load into the computer a word-processor program called SHRDLU, and that this file is in the WORDS sub-directory along with other sub-directories called NEWTEXT, OLDTEXT and BITS. The normal procedure for loading and running would be to type the name SHRDLU and press RETURN, and this would be sufficient if the program happened to be in the root directory. If the program is, as in this example, in the WORDS sub-directory, then an extended filename is needed. This filename will show the pathway to the file, just as was needed in the CD command, so that it becomes \WORDS\SHRDLU, with the first backslash sign indicating that we start at the root, and the second used as a separator. If SHRDLU had been in the NEWTEXT sub-directory, you would have needed the name \ WORDS\ NEWTEXT\SHRDLU to load and run the program. This enhancement of the filename to include the pathway through the directory is used by many MS-DOS commands, though there are still some older unchanged commands that will not accept names that include paths.

There is, however, a restriction on the extent to which you can do this path specification. No path instruction from the root directory to the lowest sub-directory can use more than 63 characters, so that the number of levels is limited to eight. The name length for a sub-directory is limited to a maximum of 8 characters, and longer names will be chopped down to this limit. Most users, however, will never need to use eight levels of sub-directories even with a hard disk and certainly not with floppies.

3 The internal commands

Some of the commands of MS-DOS are internal. This means that the routines for these commands are permanently held in the memory for as long as you are using MS-DOS, and are instantly available at any time when no other program is being run. Other commands, along with programs classed as utilities, are external. These programs have to be loaded from disk and run, like any other program, in order to be used. The main difference is that running an external command is likely to require you to change disks if you are using a floppy-disk machine. In addition, if you have been running a program then it is likely that you will have to leave the program in order to run *any* MS-DOS command, internal or external. Some programs provide for a few DOS type of actions such as file copying, deletion and renaming to be carried out from within the program. Others allow either internal or external commands to be carried out by leaving the current program but retaining it in memory. When this is done, the original program is called a *parent* and the new program that is to be run (such as an internal or external MS-DOS command) is the *child*. When the child program is an external command, this uses a different part of the memory, and allows you to return to your original program by typing EXIT (then press the RETURN key).

The distinction between internal and external MS-DOS routines is more rigorous for the user of floppy disks. When you want to run an external routine, you will need to have a System disk in drive A so that the program file can be loaded and run. The hard disk user can keep all of these external routines in a sub-directory so that they can be found when their names are typed. This requires that the PATH command be used, see later this chapter.

Internal Commands in alphabetical order

NOTE: Commands that refer to batch file use are covered in Chapter 4, and commands that relate to CONFIG.SYS use are covered in Chapter 6.

BREAK

Can be used alone, or followed by ON or OFF; and OFF is the default. In the OFF state, the DOS checks at intervals for the `Ctrl-C` or `Ctrl-Break` key combination being used. This checking is done *only* when the keyboard is in use, or when data is being sent to the screen or to the printer. When BREAK ON is used, this checking is done during other computing actions, even disk actions. This allows a program to be stopped at almost any time, and is particularly useful when a program is being tested. Using BREAK ON slows program operation because of the need to carry out the checking more often. If BREAK is used by itself, it will report the current state of BREAK.

Example
BREAK   produces on screen:
BREAK is off

– reporting that extended use of BREAK is off, so that `Ctrl-Break` or `Ctrl-C` will act only during keyboard or screen use.

Example
BREAK ON

– switches extended Break checking on, so that using `Ctrl-Break` or `Ctrl-C` will interrupt almost any action.

CHCP

Can be used alone or followed by a code page number in DOS 3.3 onwards. For an IBM system that uses code pages to accommodate printers and screen displays for different alphabets, CHCP will choose the code page for each device. For more details of code pages, see Chapter 6. CHCP cannot be used unless NLSFUNC (an external command) has been used once (possibly in the AUTOEXEC.BAT file).

Example
NLSFUNC   produces on screen the message:
Active code page: 850

– reporting that the active code page is 850, the multilingual page.

Example
CHCP 437

sets the code page to 437, the older US English page.

CHDIR or CD

Displays or changes current directory. Used alone (or followed by drive letter only) will display the current directory path that is being used in that drive. CD followed by a drive letter can be used to show the current path in a drive that is not being used at present (there must be a disk in the drive). When CD is followed by a path, it will change from the current directory to the directory at the end of the path. If the required directory branches from the current directory, do *not* begin the path with a backslash. If the required directory is on another set of branches from the root, the path *must* start with the backslash and show the path from the root.

Note: The versions CHDIR and CD are completely interchangeable.

Wildcards cannot be used with CD – you will get a Bad file name message if you try to use a wildcard.

Example
CD   producing on screen:
C:\wordproc\book\new

– will show that the path to the current directory on the current disk is as illustrated on drive C.

Example
CD B: producing on screen:
B:\copies

– will show the current path on drive B when the current drive is A or C.

Example
CD next\last

– will make the current directory LAST, assuming that LAST branches from NEXT which in turn branches from the directory which is currently being used.

Example
CD \ACCT\SPREAD\OLDFILE

– which will start at the root, then take the path of sub-directories in the order shown, ending in OLDFILE.

CLS

Clears the screen and restores normal video (bright on dark) display. A few PC machines require the line:

```
DEVICE=ANSI.SYS
```

to be placed in the CONFIG.SYS file (see Chapter 6) before CLS can be used.

COPY

A multi-purpose command which can copy files to disk, to screen or printer, alter date and time of files, or can combine files into one single copy.

1 Copying one disk file to another

This can be done either retaining the name, or with renaming. The basic form of the command is:

```
COPY SOURCE DESTINATION
```

with the files SOURCE and DESTINATION specified. The words must be separated by at least one space. If no destination filename is used, the current directory and drive is assumed; but this must *not* be where the source file is located – you cannot copy a file to its own drive and directory. If only a drive letter or path is shown as the destination, the file is copied using the same name. A wildcard can be used in the name and the first file to fit the description will be copied.

Example
```
COPY A:oldata.txt
```

– if the current drive is B:, this will copy the file OLDATA.TXT from the A: drive to the B: drive, using the same filename.

Example
```
COPY A:OLDWORK.DTA C:\OLDSTUFF
```

– will copy the file called OLDWORK.DTA into the OLDSTUFF subdirectory on drive C:, using the same name.

Example
```
COPY B:*.TXT C:\TEXTFILE
```

– will copy the first file with extension TXT on the

disk in drive B to the directory TEXTFILE in drive C. If both a destination drive or path *and* filename are typed, the file will be copied and renamed.

Example
```
COPY A:OLDTEXT.DOC C:\REWORK\NEWONE.DOC
```

– will copy the file called OLDTEXT.DOC from drive A to the subdirectory REWORK on the C: drive, and rename this file as NEWONE.DOC.

Wildcards can be used in order to copy and change the names of a number of similar files.

Example
```
COPY A:OLD?.* C:\NEWSET\NEW?.*
```

– will copy files such as OLD1.TXT, OLD2.BAT, OLD3.DOC and so on to the files NEW1.TXT, NEW2.BAT, NEW3.DOC, in which the new files take the same value for the wildcardcharacters as applied to each of the old files.

When these copies are made, the directory entry for the copied file shows the original date and time of creation. The date and time can be altered as part of the copying process by adding +,, to the *source filename* in the copy command, except when the copy is being made to the current drive, when only the + is needed. This form of the COPY command cannot usefully employ wildcards, because only the date and time of the first file that is copied will be changed.

Example
```
COPY A:OLDFILE.DOC+,, C:\NEWSTUFF
```

– will copy OLDFILE.DOC into the subdirectory NEWSTUFF, and change the date and time information to the date and time of copying.

Example
```
COPY A:DATAFIL.TXT+
```

– will copy DATAFIL.TXT from the A: drive to the current drive and change the date and time to the date and time of copying.

2 Copying to/from devices.

The use of device names was introduced with V.2.0. A device, in this context, means screen, serial port, or printer, and MS-DOS allows another device called NUL which will simply do nothing with a file. NUL is a way of preventing a message from being seen in some circumstances, or for testing that a COPY command will work, without the need to wait for anything to be copied. The Device abbreviations are:

CON for the monitor screen *and* keyboard.
PRN or LPT1 for the printer
NUL for the Null device.

Note: The letters AUX or COM1 are used for the serial port, but COPY will not necessarily receive *from* this device, although it can send ASCII text (no Crtl characters) *to* the serial port.

COPY is used with device names usually to send a file to the screen or printer, but it can also be used to cause text to be copied from the keyboard to a disk file or direct to the printer. When a disk file is created in this way, the copy action runs until the key combinations Ctrl-C or Ctrl-Break are pressed. When copying is used from keyboard to printer, the end of each line must be signalled with Ctrl-N before the RETURN key is pressed on the line, and the printing is done when Ctrl-Z is pressed, and then the RETURN key.

Example
COPY A:LETTER1.DOC PRN

– will copy the file LETTER1.DOC to the printer. A wildcardcan be used in the filename if you are not sure of the precise name. The file must be in ASCII code, and this means that files made by many well-known word-processors will produce strange effects, depending on the type of printer, because of the use of codes in the range 128 to 255, or in the range 1 to 31. Most word-processors have an option that allows files to be recorded in ASCII form (or permit a print to a disk file), and another solution is to pipe the file through a filter program which will correct the characters into ASCII codes. See Chapter 6 for details of using pipes and filters.

Example
COPY C:\OLDTEXT\LET5.DOC CON

– will copy the file LET5.DOC, in the OLDTEXT subdirectory, to the screen. A wildcardcan be used in the filename.

Example
COPY CON C:BOLDPRNT.BAT

– will copy whatever you type on the keyboard into

a file called BOLDPRNT.BAT until you press the `Ctrl-C` (or `Ctrl-Break`) keys.

Example
`COPY CON PRN`

– will copy what you type on the keyboard to the printer when you finally press `Ctrl-Z` and then RETURN. The end of a printed line must be marked with `Ctrl-N`.

3 To combine files

The source files are shown following the COPY command word in order, using the + sign between each pair. The destination file is shown in the usual way. Source files can be taken from any disk or directory provided that no disk changing is needed during the copy action (though it *is* possible to swap the disk in one drive while a file is being copied from another drive).

Example
`COPY A:FILE1.DOC+C:\OLDBITS\FILE2.TXT C:\`
`NEWBITS\NEWONE.TXT`

– will copy FILE1.DOC from the A: drive, and then append the file FILE2.TXT from the OLDBITS directory, naming the new file NEWONE.TXT and placing it in the NEWONE directory. Note that there *must be no space* on either side of the + sign.

This form of COPY will also take a wildcard-description, so that it can be used to join a number of files with a very compact command.

Example
`COPY A:+NOTE?.* B:TOTAL.TXT`

– can be used to join files in the A: drive, called NOTE1.TXT, NOTE2.DOC, NOTE3.WRD and NOTE4.ADD into one file called TOTAL.TXT on the B: drive.

COPY options

The COPY command allows three option letters `A`, `B` and `V` to be used. Of these, `V` is the most useful, as it causes the copy to be verified, with an error report if there is any difference between the original and the copy. This is equivalent in action to the VERIFY command, and its use will slow down COPY actions.

Example
```
COPY A:PRECIOUS.TXT C:\VALUE/V
```

– will copy the file called PRECIOUS from the A drive to the subdirectory called VALUE on the C drive, and will then verify that the copy is correct.

The A and B options are intended to specify ASCII and Binary files respectively. The difference is that an ASCII file of text has its end marked with the Ctrl-Z character, code 26, but a binary file must always be copied until the last byte, as indicated by the length of the file number, has been dealt with. If these options are not used, COPY assumes a binary action for any straightforward copying of files, and an ASCII action when files are being combined.

Example
```
COPY A:TXTFIL.DOC/A B:
```

– will copy TXTFIL.DOC from drive A to drive B, copying everything in TXTFIL up to the end-of-file byte, code 26. This byte is *not* copied to the B drive, so that the file copy will *not* be identical. Subsequent uses of COPY will be ASCII copies unless the /B option is specified.

Example
```
COPY A:TXTFIL.DOC/A B:/A
```

– will copy TXTFIL.DOC from drive A to drive B, and will copy the end-of-file byte also. Subsequent copies will be ASCII copies unless the /B option is specified.

Example
```
COPY A:PROGRAM.COM/B B:
```

– will copy the binary (program) file PROGRAM.COM from drive A to drive B, treating this as a binary file. The /B option is needed only if a previous use of COPY employed the /A option. There will be an end-of-file byte added to the copy, so that the copy is not identical to the original.

Example
```
COPY A:PROG.EXE/B B:/B
```

– will copy the binary file PROG.EXE from drive A to drive B, with no end of file marker on the copy. This is required only if a previous COPY command used ASCII options on both files.

CTTY

This is a command that is used to pass control of the computer from the keyboard, usually to something that is connected to the serial input. The 'something' can be an auxiliary keyboard or another computer, and when CTTY has been used, this other device has *complete* control, allowing MS-DOS commands to be entered and executed. Once CTTY has been used to pass command, only the remote device can return command by issuing another CTTY command, other than by re-booting the PC machine. To disconnect, assuming a remote computer has control, CTTY CON must be typed on the remote machine.

Example
CTTY AUX1

– will hand over command to the serial input, which must be connected to a serial keyboard or to the serial port of another computer. Your machine will lock up if there is nothing suitable connected.

Example
CTTY CON

– will restore the normal use of the keyboard on the main machine. In general CTTY is little-used, because it's generally more useful to run communications software when you communicate with other computers.

DATE

This allows the date to be set in the internal clock of the computer. Normally you would set the correct date, but there is nothing wrong in setting another date if you feel this might be useful. One application of setting an incorrect date is to avoid Friday 13th being used, since some viruses are activated on this date. The older type of PC machine required the date (and time) to be set each time the computer was switched on, but most modern machines use a battery-backed clock circuit that requires no re-setting except for the change to and from Summer Time. When batteries need to be changed on such machines, they can be changed while the machine is switched on, so that the date and time information is not lost.

The form of the DATE command is DATE alone, which prints the date and asks for you to alter this if you want (press RETURN to leave it alone, or type a date and then press RETURN; or DATE followed by a date, which will enter that date. Date format is determined by the country-file of MS-DOS, and for the UK is DD-MM-YY. If you keep finding dates like 6–23–89 then you are using the US country setting in which dates are written in MM-DD-YY order. If the entered date is not valid (wrong format or an impossible date) you will be prompted to enter a corrected version.

Example
DATE

– prints the date on screen, and asks if any update is needed.

Example
DATE 05-02-89

– makes the date 5th February 1989 for a computer that uses UK date conventions.

DEL (or ERASE)

Either DEL or ERASE can be used to delete files, either single files or, using a wildcard, in groups. If the use of DEL or ERASE would result in deleting all the files on a disk or in a directory, you will be asked to confirm the command by typing Y or N. DEL (ERASE) *cannot* be used to delete a directory, for which the RD command is used.

Example
DEL arcturus.008

– will delete the single file on the current drive/directory with this name

Example
DEL A:*.TXT

– will delete all files with the extension letters TXT on the A: drive.

Example
DEL B:*.*

– will delete all files on the disk in the B: drive. You will be asked to confirm that you really intend this to be done with the message:

    Are you sure (Y/N)

and the files will be deleted only if you answer Y. Using N or any other letter will leave the files as they are.

Note that the file(s) that deleted using DEL or ERASE in this way are not in fact removed or replaced in the disk unless other files are recorded over them. If a file or set of files is deleted by mistake, then follow the following procedure:

1 If the files were on a floppy disk, make a backup copy of the disk on to a new formatted disk using the DISKCOPY utility (which will copy the deleted files as well). The computer can then be used with other disks. If the files were on the hard disk, then *do not save* any other files on to the hard disk. Continue work on floppy disks if possible.

2 Load in a disk utility program which will restore deleted files. Programs such as PC-Tools Plus, Norton's Utilities or Ultra Utilities are ideal for this purpose. Follow the instructions for the particular file recovery program that you are using. The important point is not to record any more data on the disk which would replace the files that have been deleted in error. For some file types, such as text files, it is possible to recover the remaining data if another file has been recorded over the deleted file, but only the portion that has not been over-written can be recovered.

Note that if you have more serious problems with file loss, particularly from a hard disk, which cannot be treated by the use of file recovery programs, then there are specialists, such as Alan Solomon, of S & S Enterprises Ltd. (see advertisements in Personal Computer World magazine) who can recover data under remarkably adverse conditions. These services are expensive, but if a set of files represents a year's work, the price is reasonable.

DIR

DIR is the directory command, the method of finding what files are contained on a disk or a directory. It can be used to display all files, details of one file or a group answering to a wildcarddescription, or to test if a file or set of files is present. The command word can be used alone, followed by a drive or path or by a complete file specification, and can be modified by the letters P or W.

The most general use is to list all files, so that the command applies to the current drive, and consists only of DIR.

Example
DIR

– this produces a display such as:

```
Volume in drive A has no label
Directory of A:\
PCSCAP  TXT    384 29-01-89 18:56
PDS1    TXT  18944 31-01-89  9:33
PDS2    TXT  23424 31-01-89 15:02
PDS3    TXT   8448 31-01-89 15:03
PDS4    TXT    896 29-01-89 18:54
PDS5    TXT    768 29-01-89 18:55
PDS6    TXT    640 29-01-89 18:55
PDS7    TXT    640 29-01-89 18:55
PDS8    TXT    640 29-01-89 18:56
PDSAPP  TXT    384 29-01-89 18:56
PDSPRF  TXT   2048 30-01-89 11:30
11 File(s)    301056 bytes free
```

which shows the files that are present on this drive, along with the label name, if any, and the amount of disk space that is free for use. The files are shown one on each line as a default mainly because the original PC machine used a 40-character per line screen display, and a modification to the COMMAND.COM file will allow two-column display as a default.

Two-column display is useful because it allows the display of more files before the screen scrolls, and another way of achieving two-column display is to use DIR/W which will give filenames and extensions only, with no file sizes, dates or times. If the directory contains a large number of files, using DIR/P will *page* the file list, so that the screen shows 24 lines and holds this information until any key is pressed, when the next 24 lines will be shown. The /W and /P options can be used on any DIR display.

Example
DIR/W

– will show the directory display in two columns as shown in Figure 3.1.

```
Volume in drive A has no label

Directory of A:\

PCSCAP  TXT    384 29-01-89 18:56   PDS1    TXT  18944 31-01-89  9:33
PDS2    TXT  23424 31-01-89 15:02   PDS3    TXT   8448 31-01-89 15:03
PDS4    TXT    896 29-01-89 18:54   PDS5    TXT    768 29-01-89 18:55
PDS6    TXT    640 29-01-89 18:5    PDS7    TXT    640 29-01-89 18:55
PDS8    TXT    640 29-01-89 18:56   PDSAPP  TXT    384 29-01-89 18:56
PDSPRF  TXT   2048 30-01-89 11:30
       11 File(s)     301056 bytes free
```

Figure 3.1

Example
DIR A:/P

- will show a directory of drive A on screen, printing the entries one to a line until 23 lines are displayed. The message at the bottom of the screen is:

Press a key when ready...

and when a key is pressed, the next 23 lines of the directory listing will be displayed. The DIR command can also specify a drive or a path other than the current one.

Example
DIR B:

- will give the directory of the B: drive when the current drive is the A: drive, and A: will still be the current drive *after* the command has been run.

Example
DIR C:\OLDPROG\TYPEWORD

-will give the list of files for a directory called TYPEWORD that is a branch from OLDPROG on the C: disk. DIR can be used to give details of one file that is known to exist on a drive or a directory.

Example
DIR C:\ODDS\MYFILE.TXT

- will show the details of the file MYFILE.TXT, assuming that it exists. If the file does not exist, an error message will be displayed.

DIR is very often used with wildcards, but it does not need to have a wildcardcharacter typed if either the main name or the extension is to be substituted.

Example
DIR A:FILE

- is equivalent to DIR A:FILE.* and it will display all files on the A: drive with the filename FILE, but with different extensions.

Example
DIR B:.BAT

- is equivalent to DIR B:*.BAT and will display any file that has the extension letters of BAT on the B: drive.

DIR will also display a directory if one exists on a disk, or inside another directory. When a name in a listing is a directory, the DIR listing shows the name but with 〈DIR〉 inside angled brackets following it rather than the usual size, date and time details. This allows you to use the CD command to move to that directory if required, or to use a DIR command that includes the directory in order to find what files are contained in the directory. A directory listing can also be *redirected* to a disk file or to the printer, see Chapter 6.

Example
DIR/W   See Figure 3.2

- with several directories shown in this portion of a directory listing.

MKDIR or MD

This command, always used in its abbreviated form, makes a new sub-directory, and is mainly intended for hard-disk use. The sub-directory name follows the MD command, and the directory that is created is always a branch from the current directory.

Example
MD NEWDIR

- makes NEWDIR a new subdirectory. If at the time of using MD the current path was C:\ PROGSET\DIRS then the path to the new directory is C:\PROGSET\DIRS\NEWDIR. A new directory can be created from another branch by including path data in the specification, starting from the root.

Example
MD C:\FILES\LETTERS\OLDLET

- will create a new directory called OLDLET which is a branch from LETTERS which in turn is a branch of FILES on the root directory.

PATH

When a program name is typed, and then RETURN pressed, MS-DOS will look for a file with that name and extensions of COM, EXE (or, finally, BAT) on the current drive or directory. If the file does not exist on the current drive or directory, then the File not found message will be issued. By using a PATH command, MS-DOS can be instructed to search other drives and/or directories for programs, with the order

```
COMMAND  COM    23612  14-07-86  12:13    SR       COM     4890  1-01-80   0:00
AUTOEXEC BAK      139   7-02-89  10:56    XTREE    EXE    43280  18-12-85  0:03
ANSI     SYS     1699  14-07-86  12:13    DTP      BAT      296  2-02-89  17:29
DRIVER   SYS     1110  14-07-86  12:13    RAMDRIVE SYS     6566  14-07-86 12:13
XTREEINS EXE     8968   3-11-85   9:33    XTREEINS DAT    20608  3-11-85   9:33
WDPARK   EXE     9424   9-09-87  14:37    SCRUTLS  <DIR>         4-02-88  15:54
MSDOS    <DIR>          4-02-88  13:57    WSTAR    <DIR>         4-02-88  14:19
EDITORS  <DIR>          4-02-88  14:21    LIBFIL   <DIR>         4-02-88  17:11
LOTUS    <DIR>          8-11-88  14:18    COMMS    <DIR>         4-02-88  14:59
TEXTUTIL <DIR>          4-02-88  15:03    LANG     <DIR>         4-02-88  15:30
```

Figure 3.2

of search being specified. PATH is used to determine what pathways are given preference in MS-DOS when *program* files (EXE and COM files) are being searched for. The use of floppy disks does not need to use PATH, because each program disk will be inserted in order to run the program. On a hard disk, however, you may need to run a program while you are working in a sub-directory. As before, you will get an error message if the program file cannot be found. PATH, typed alone as a command, will display whatever paths exist.

Example
PATH   producing on screen:
C:\MSDOS;C:\OTHERS

– means that when a program name is typed, the current drive or directory will be searched, then a directory in the C: drive called MSDOS, and if the program is not found in this set, a directory called OTHERS which is also in the C: drive.

Following PATH by a semicolon alone clears a previous PATH commands, so that PATH; would result in only the current drive/directory being searched the next time a program name is typed.

To create a new path, the PATH line must be typed and RETURN pressed before a program is requested. Each path must start with a root directory of any disk, and each path is separated from the next by a semicolon. The usual place for a PATH command is the AUTOEXEC.BAT file (see Chapter 4), but it can be used alone or in other batch files.

Example
PATH C:\LANGS\EDITORS;C:\WORDS;C:\TEXT

– would result in a search being made of the current drive/directory, then the EDITORS subdirectory of LANGS, then the WORDS directory, then the TEXT directory.

PROMPT

is used to change the normal prompt from the form:

A>

to some other form, which can include date and time if needed. The PROMPT word can be followed by ordinary text, which will make this text into the new prompt. If PROMPT is used alone, it restores the default message. Changing the prompt message would normally be used in the AUTOEXEC.BAT file, see Chapter 4.

Example
PROMPT Type command:

will make the prompt appear as:

Type command:

rather than as simply A)

Example
PROMPT

– will restore the normal A) type of prompt.

PROMPT can also be used with a set of special characters, all preceded with the dollar sign, to place other quantities into a prompt. One of these character pairs *$e* can be used to alter screen conditions if the ANSI.SYS file has been used in the CONFIG.SYS file, see Chapter 6. The special characters are:

\$b the $ character
\$d the current date
\$e the ESC character (ASCII 27)
\$g the) character
\$h backspace and erase previous character
\$l the (character (note letter ell, not number 1)
\$n the current default drive
\$p the current drive/directory path
\$q the = character
\$t the current time
\$v the MS-DOS version number
\$\$ the $ sign
\$_ the new-line character
\$ the carriage-return and new-line characters

Any other characters following the dollar sign are ignored by the PROMPT command.

Example
PROMPT pg   produces on screen:
C:\DIR1\DIR2)

Example
PROMPT $d $t $n $g   produces on screen:
Fri 17–02–1989 13:36:18.54 C)

at the time when this command was issued.

REN (or RENAME)

is used to change the name of a file, or a group of files if a suitable wildcard is used. A directory does *not* count as a file in this respect, and cannot be renamed by using the REN command. There is no provision in MS-DOS for renaming a directory, but there are utilities which will carry out this action, and an alternative is to create a new directory of the desired new name and transfer all the files across, using COPY with a wildcard. The normal use of REN allows for a wildcard character in both oldname and newname.

Example
REN A:OLDFILE.TXT OLDFILE.BAK

renames the extension of OLDFILE, retaining the main name.

Example
REN A:*.TXT *.BAK

– will change all TXT extensions to BAK extensions

Example
REN C:\FIRST\FILEA.DOC FILEB.DOC

– renames FILEA.DOC to FILEB.DOC, and there is no need to repeat the path information for the new name, since REN does not copy data. If the same path is included, the renaming will be carried out normally. If you attempt to use a different path in the new name, REN will stop with an error message of Invalid parameter.

Example
REN TEXT?.TXT CHAP?.TXT

– will convert TEXT1.TXT to CHAP1.TXT, TEXT2.TXT to CHAP2.TXT and so on

RMDIR (or RD)

The shortened form is normally used, and the effect is to remove a directory from a branch or root. The command must be followed by the path and name of the directory (no wildcards), and there must be *no* files contained in the directory. The directory must not contain any further sub-directories, and it must not be assigned to a spare drive letter (see ASSIGN, Chapter 5). No directory can be removed if it is the current directory.

Example
```
RD C:TEXTOLDTEXT
```

– will remove the OLDTEXT directory if it is empty and is not the current directory.

Example
```
RD OLDTEXT
```

– will remove the OLDTEXT directory, when the current directory is the TEXT directory and the OLDTEXT directory is empty.

SET

is used to set 'environment variables'. These are assignments that can be made in advance of running a program that uses them, and the assignments are stored in a piece of memory (normally 160 bytes) that is set aside for this use. If you attempt to store too much in this space, you will get the ominous error message `Out of environment space`. The amount of environment space can be increased by using a SHELL line in the CONFIG.SYS file, see Chapter 6. The use of SET depends on the programs that you run, and may not be necessary for many of your programs. The form of the command is SET name = text, where the name is one that will be used to pass the text to a program. There *must not* be any space on either side of the = sign.

The environment settings are stored as ASCII codes in the portion of memory that is set aside for them, with each string terminated by a zero. The end of the last string is marked with two zeros. SET, used alone, will print on screen all of the existing environmental settings. Usually these will include COMSPEC, the file that has to be used for commands (usually COMMAND.COM) and PATH, showing the PATH set in the AUTOEXEC.BAT file. Using a line such as:

```
SET THISNAME=
```

with nothing following the equality sign will reset the use of THISNAME, so that this no longer appears in the SET list. For using environment parameters in batch files, see Chapter 4.

Example
SET COMSPEC=C:\COMMAND.COM

– will ensure that MSDOS will search drive C root directory for COMMAND.COM when this has to be re-loaded after being overlaid with a program.

Example
SET TMP=D:\

– means that a program which uses TMP to represent temporary storage space can make use of a RAMdisk that has been set up as drive D:

Example
SET PATH=C:\COMPILE

– means that a program which uses PATH to define where it will look for programs will use C:\ COMPILE rather than follow the paths that have been set up in a PATH command.

Example
SET

– will print on screen all the present settings of environment variables.

Example
SET EVNVAR=

– will cancel any assignment to the variable ENVVAR.

TIME

is used to set the computer clock, or to report the current time. When TIME is used, the current time will be printed, and you can then type in a correction, in the form that is specified for your country. For the UK set, this is usually HH:MM. Time is not set using seconds, but when the RETURN key is pressed the seconds figure is assumed to be zero.

Example
TIME

– gives the current time, and asks you to enter a new time. Press RETURN if you do not want to change the time.

Example
TIME 15:15

– changes the current time to 3.15 p.m. The setting is made when the RETURN key is pressed on the typed time number, so that it is possible to synchronize the setting to the seconds hand of a watch or to telephone or TV time signals.

TYPE

is the command that allows a file to be copied to the screen, so that its action is equivalent to that of COPY filename PRN. TYPE must be followed by a valid filename, which can include a drive, a path, main filename and extension. Wildcards are completely ignored, and if you attempt to use a wildcardyou will get an error message File not found. Only ASCII files are suitable for use with TYPE, because TYPE filters out characters in the range 0 to 31 that cannot be displayed. In addition, because TYPE is intended for ASCII files, the presence of the ASCII end-of-file character (code 26) will end the use of TYPE on a file. The extended character set (codes 129 to 255) is shown, however, so that output from WordStar, or any other source of text in which some ASCII characters have 128 added to the code number (the 7th bit set) will show as characters in various European alphabets, or as mathematical symbols.

TYPE does not page its text, so that the screen scrolls continuously. The scrolling can be halted by pressing Ctrl-S or Ctrl-NumLock, and restarted by pressing Ctrl-Q, though on some computers, *any* single key will restart scrolling, and some keys have the unfortunate effect of inhibiting the Ctrl-S effect, so that scrolling cannot be stopped again. Using Ctrl-C or Ctrl-Break will end the display. The lack of paging can be overcome by using the MORE filter (more useful for hard-disk users), see Chapter 6. As an alternative, there are several screen-display utilities available that allow paging and also the ability to browse through a document, scrolling backwards as well as forwards. Many such utilities are available as public domain programs, but several are fairly old and do not necessarily accept filenames with directory paths. All of these versions of TYPE are external programs.

If each page shown by TYPE is to be printed, press Ctrl-P or Ctrl-PrtSc before pressing RETURN on the type command, and again after the TYPE session has finished. In general, it is more satisfactory to use COPY filename PRN than to use TYPE for printing files in this way.

Example
TYPE C:\WORDS\FILE1.DOC

– will display the file FILE1.DOC on the screen, showing all of the ASCII codes present in the file and scrolling the screen as it fills up. Ctrl-S stops the scrolling, Ctrl-Q restarts it, and Ctrl-C (or Ctrl-Break) ends the action.

Example
TYPE A:READ.ME then press Ctrl-P then RETURN

– will print the file and also show it on screen. The printer *must* be ready to use before this command is issued. After typing the file, Ctrl-P must be pressed again, otherwise everything that typed will be echoed to the printer and if the printer is switched off, the computer will appear to lock up. To release such a lock, switch the printer on, press Ctrl-P, and then switch the printer off again.

VER

is used to print on the screen the version of MS-DOS that is currently being used

Example
VER   on my computer produces
MS-DOS Version 3.20

VERIFY

has to be followed by ON or OFF. When VERIFY ON has been used, any file that is saved on a disk will be checked to ensure that the disk copy is identical. The checking is *not* character-by-character, but the sum of ASCII codes of characters (a checksum) so that it is possible that the copy might be incorrect due to two errors cancelling each other out, but this is most unlikely.

Using VERIFY ON will certainly detect the effect of trying to record over a faulty sector on a hard or floppy disk. Using VERIFY OFF turns off the checking, and VERIFY, typed alone, will indicate whether VERIFY is on or off. VERIFY is normally OFF, and can be switched on by using VERIFY ON in the AUTOEXEC.BAT file (see Chapter 4). *Note* that no messages are delivered unless a disk save is faulty, so that you do not normally know whether VERIFY is on or off. The VERIFY action is the same as that used for the /V option of the COPY command.

Example
VERIFY   shows on screen:
VERIFY is off

Example
VERIFY ON

– will switch on verification for file copying.

VOL

is used to print on screen the label of a disk (see LABEL, Chapter 5), which is the name of up to 11 characters that you give to the disk. This applies mainly to floppy disks, and allows you to recognize your disks even if any paper labels have dropped off from the outside. It has little applicability to hard disk use. The label name is also displayed when the DIR command is used.

Example
VOL

– displays label of disk in current drive.

Example
VOL B:

– displays label of disk in another drive.

4 Batch files and commands

When you use the computer DOS commands directly, each action requires you to type a command and then press the RETURN key so that the command is carried out at once. This type of use is often called interactive, and the alternative is called batch use, in which you issue a set of commands and then let the computer get on with the job of carrying out each one in sequence. Obviously, the commands have to be typed in rather a different way in order to achieve this, because what you are doing is to write a miniature program of commands that are intended to be executed later and in a particular order. This is done in MS-DOS, much as it is done in other operating systems, by writing a file that is recorded on to a disk. This file is called a *batch file*, and by typing the name of such a batch file, you can make the computer carry out the commands that are contained in the file.

Suppose, for example, that you had a batch file recorded on a disk under the filename BAKELIM.BAT . We can imagine that the purpose of this batch file is to delete certain files with a BAK extension, but only certain files. If we wanted to eliminate all files with a BAK extension, it would be much easier just to use DEL *.BAK, but anything that involves picking and choosing along with repetition is an ideal candidate for a batch file. With the batch file present on the current drive (or on a suitable path), all you need to do is to type BAKELIM, the name of the batch file. You might, of course, if you have twin drives, keep all of your batch files on one disk that you place in drive A and make the commands operate on files that are kept in whatever disk is placed in drive B. Users of hard disks can keep all of the batch files in the root directory so as to make it easy to select programs by means of batch files, a use that will be illustrated later.

Example

```
DEL FIRST.BAK
DEL SECND.BAK
LABEL DEMODISK
```
(saved under the name BAKELIM)

When this runs, it will delete the files FIRST.BAK

and SECND.BAK, then label the disk as DEMODISK. If one or more files cannot be found, this will be reported, but the batch file will then continue with the following instruction.

Creating a batch file

A batch file is simply a set of commands, recorded in ASCII codes, and with one command on each line of the file. No special end-of-text character needs to be placed in the file, because a file editor will insert this for you. You can create batch files with the EDLIN editing program that is on the system disk. This, however, is not an easy program to use, and a simple text editor, such as the RPED program that is supplied with Amstrad machines is very much easier to use. There is a huge choice of such editors in the public domain, see Appendix D.

Another method is to prepare the text of a batch file with a word-processor which allows you to create ASCII files (called non-document files in WordStar). Yet another method is to type COPY CON filename which will save everything you type to a file, using whatever you typed as the filename, when you type Ctrl-Z and RETURN at the end of the file. The batch file consists of the usual commands of MS-DOS, plus a few very useful commands that are peculiar to batch files, and which make the batch file much more like a programming language in its own right. Some of the commands can be used independently in MS-DOS command lines as distinct from batch files. Each batch file must use the extension letters BAT, since this identifies it as a batch file when you look at the disk directory. The fact that the file has this extension also allows the machine to locate the file when you type the main filename. If you do not use the extension BAT, then the file will simply be treated like any other file of text, not as a batch file.

A batch file must *never* carry the same name as is used for a file of the COM or EXE type, such as COMMAND.BAT. This is because when a batch file name is used, the BAT suffix is not typed, and the machine will search first for COM or EXE files of this name, and subsequently for batch files. Any name that is the name of a COM or EXE file will cause that COM or EXE file to be run in preference to the batch file.

Autoexec.bat

Another important point is that there is a very special reserved name for a batch file, AUTOEXEC.BAT. If you have a file of that name on any disk which contains the DOS tracks (a start-of-day disk or boot disk), then whatever is contained in this batch file will be carried out automatically after the machine has read the DOS and before it is ready for use by you. This can save a considerable amount of time if you had previously started a computing session by issuing a set of commands for such purposes as, for example, preparing the printer for use, clearing a disk, copying, renaming or deleting files and so on. By putting all of these actions into an AUTOEXEC.BAT file, you are saved both the effort of carrying out the actions and the equal effort of remembering which actions are needed for which disk.

You might, for example, want all of your word-processing disks to carry one form of printer setup, and all your spreadsheet disks to carry another. It's likely, too, that any programs that you buy will have AUTOEXEC.BAT files, and you may want to look at these files (using TYPE) and possibly modify them to suit your own purposes. The use of AUTOEXEC.BAT files is essential for hard-disk users, and several examples will be given later in this chapter.

Using BATCH files

There are no restrictions on the number of BAT files that you may have on your disk (subject to available space) or how you make use of them provided that the commands are valid. If some commands are not valid, then you will get an error message, but this does *not* stop the batch file from running. For example, if you repeat the use of the batch file example BAKELIM on the same disk as you tested it on, then you will get 'File not found' for each of the DEL commands, but the LABEL action will be repeated, and the whole batch file is carried out. It can be very useful to keep several batch files on a disk, so that you have choices of actions. If you want to end the action of a batch file while it is running, press the Ctrl-C or Ctrl-Break keys. You will get the message:

`Terminate Batch job (Y/N)?`

and answering with Y will end the use of the batch file. You *must* ensure that the disk with the batch file is present in the current drive or in a drive/directory that can be searched. If the batch file cannot be found, you will see the message:

`Insert disk with batch file`
`and press any key when ready`

which means that the machine cannot find the batch file that it has been working on. This is more likely to happen when batch files are used from floppy disks, and running a program as directed by a batch file requires you to replace the disk with the batch file by one containing a program. When batch files are used on a hard disks, they should either be placed in the root directory or in a directory that is indicated in a PATH command (see Chapter 3).

On a floppy system, since the filenames can refer to other drive(s), the batch file disk need not necessarily be the disk that is used to hold the files that are operated on, but the disk containing the batch file *must* be present while the batch file actions are being carried out. If you use several batch files on one disk, you should try to make the filenames remind you of the action. For example, names like SETPRN, SCRNCOL or CHARLIN can remind you of batch files that set the printer (margins, bold face, 40 characters per line for book or magazine listings, for example), the screen colours for foreground and background, and the number of characters per line on the screen. Using a hard disk system, the batch files should preferably be held in the root directory, and it is possible to make each of the batch files carry out the selection and running of a program, including all the selection of directories, any SET actions, and the running of any preliminary programs (to set up the mouse or printer, for example) that might be needed. Such batch files can also be used to return control to the root directory after use. Using batch files in this way is considerably easier, cheaper and less demanding of memory than the use of mouse/ icon 'front-end' programs.

Example

```
echo off
echo Juki printer must be used
```

```
pause
cd\prnutil
typit2
cd
```

In this example (the ECHO lines will be explained later), the CD\PRNUTIL command selects the correct directory, and the next line runs the program (a routine to use the printer and keyboard like a typewriter; useful for filling in forms). When the TYPIT2 program is ended, the final CD\ returns to the root directory. An improvement here would be to follow this with the line:

```
DIR *.BAT
```

which would show on screen all of the other batch files which were available for use.

Though you can have as many BAT files as you please, subject to overall memory, you can have only one AUTOEXEC.BAT file. This is run automatically when the machine is booted, but there is no prohibition on running it at a later time by typing the name AUTOEXEC, though this is seldom necessary except possibly to restore the use of a program that was run in this way and whose action has been cancelled by running another program.

Specialized commands

In their simplest form, batch files are an extremely useful method of selecting and running programs with minimal effort, but their real strength comes when the full set of batch commands can be used. For the more advanced user, a batch file can be almost a miniature program in its own right, dealing with a complex set of commands on files that can, of course, include such points as redirection, pipes and filters (see Chapter 6). The most useful of the more advanced batch techniques, however, involves the use of % parameters. A parameter in this sense means something like the name of a disk file, something that is used in the batch file, but is not the same each time that the batch file is used. For example, you might make a batch file that consisted of the two commands:

```
DEL TEXT.BAK
RENAME TEXT.TXT  OLDTEXT.TXT
```

– and this would be a perfectly valid batch file for a disk that contained files of these names.

You might, however, have disks on which you had files of other names, but always with the requirement to delete one file and rename another. One way out of the problem is to use names that stand-in for the actual names, so that the commands implied that you should delete file number 1 and rename file number 2 to name number 3. This is just about the form of a general-purpose batch file command. The % sign is used to mean name number, so that the commands would appear as:

```
DEL %1
RENAME %2 %3
```

The significance of the numbers is that they show the *order* of names that you would have to supply following the name of the batch file. In the original example, if we imagine that this batch file has been recorded with the filename of FRUIT.BAT, then by typing:

```
FRUIT TEXT.BAK TEXT.TXT OLDTEXT.TXT
```

– you would ensure that the filename TEXT.BAK is used in the %1 position, the file TEXT.TXT in the %2 position, and the file OLDTEXT.TXT in the %3 position. This in turn would ensure that TEXT.BAK is deleted, and TEXT.TXT is renamed as OLDTEXT.TXT. Though you can use these reference numbers for up to ten items (numbers 0 to 9), it is not essential to use all of them provided that you leave no gaps in the list. Omitting a name may lead to an error message, as when the machine is asked to delete a file whose name is not supplied, but this does not stop the batch file. For example, if you have a call to a batch file such as:

```
DOIT %1 %2 %3
```

then omitting the third name will cause no problems, nor will omitting the second and third names, or even all of the names. You cannot, however, omit only the first name, or the second name, because the names are read in order. If you want to omit one action, supply a nonsense name, so that you might call this example batch file using:

```
DOIT FILE1 NONAME FILE2
```

– with no file called NONAME, but with real files

for FILE1 and FILE2.

The %1, %2 and %3 in the example are called dummy parameters, and the names that you put into the call for the batch file will be substituted in sequence. This does not mean that a name cannot be used more than once, only that the sequence of typing the names determines how they are allocated to the parameters %1, %2 and %3 in this example. You can also make use of the parameter %0, but not very often. The reason is that %0 is the first filename that you type, which is always the name of the batch file itself, FRUIT OR DOIT in these examples. For most purposes, then, you will not make any use of %0. Another point to remember is that when you type a name, such as FRUIT, MS-DOS will search for this among the EXE and COM files first, and then through the BAT files. If the name you have used is also the name of a COM or EXE file, then your batch file will never run. You can use only the parameters %1 to %9, and for most purposes this is adequate. It does not necessarily mean that you can use only ten parameters, only that ten is the maximum that can be used *at a time*. If you have used ten parameters, and need to be able to enter another set, you can re-assign parameters by using SHIFT. Each time SHIFT is used, the parameter %0 becomes available for use again, and the others are shifted by one number. This means that what used to be represented by %0 is now represented by %1, what was represented by %1 is now represented by %2, and so on, with the filename that was represented by %9 now no longer in use. It's most unlikely that you will ever need to use this facility, which I always think causes more problems than it eliminates.

One of the most valuable features of batch files is that each batch file virtually adds a new command to your MS-DOS. As far as your use of MS-DOS is concerned, typing something like MAKEWAY oldtext newtext is no different in style from typing TYPE oldtext, and its effect is to carry out some actions. You can therefore add batch files to your MS-DOS disks so that you can carry out the actions that you need most often with the minimum of typing. As noted earlier, this is particularly useful as an easy way of selecting and running programs on a hard disk, and its use is a considerable saving in time and memory (not to mention cost!) compared to the 'front-end' programs that are sold with a view to making the use of MS-DOS easier.

AUTOEXEC.BAT rules

Any file that carries the name of AUTOEXEC.BAT
is a very special file, and there must only ever be one
file with this name on a disk. You can, however, have
several floppy disks, each configured as a system disk
and each with a file called AUTOEXEC.BAT, but
with these files entirely different on each disk. The
significance of the AUTOEXEC.BAT file is that you
never have to type the name AUTOEXEC to run this
batch file unless you want to run it again. It will run
automatically on any disk that contains the MS-DOS
operating system, immediately after the operating
system has been loaded. There can only be one active
AUTOEXEC.BAT file on a hard disk, however.

Take a look, by way of introduction, at the
AUTOEXEC.BAT file on my own hard disk.

```
echo off
path c:\;C:\MSDOS;C:\editors;C:\textutil
keybuk
mouse
rtc
graphics
prtscfx
sr 200
dir *.bat
echo on
```

The ECHO OFF command is something that we'll
come to shortly – it switches off the screen copy of
each command in the batch file. This is followed by
a PATH command which shows where MS-DOS
should look for programs that are not contained in
the current sub-directory. The KEYBUK program
makes the keyboard of the (Amstrad) PC follow the
UK pattern, for example, by having the English
pound sign. The MOUSE command loads in the
MOUSE program so that the mouse can be used with
desk-top publishing and CAD programs, and RTC
ensures that the clock circuits in the Amstrad
machine can be used to set the time in programs like
Lotus 1-2-3. The GRAPHICS and PRTSCFX
programs allow graphics patterns to be printed on an
Epson dot-matrix printer – GRAPHICS is used for
graphics screens and PRTSCFX for text screens. The
SR 200 line installs a memory cache program called

SpeedRead, and allocates 200K of memory to it. Finally, the DIR *.BAT command ensures that the screen displays all of the batch files that have been written to handle the starting and ending of programs.

Floppy disk use – Example

Suppose that you copied a word-processor called SHRDLU on to a floppy disk which had been formatted as a system disk, so that it contains all of the MS-DOS tracks. Up until now, you might have been resigned to starting up MS-DOS separately, and then loading SHRDLU by typing its name. Now you can proceed differently, making an AUTOEXEC.BAT file of this form:

```
ECHO OFF
KEYBUK
SHRDLU
```

– which will ensure the use of the UK keyboard, and then run your word-processor. You need to put KEYBUK in, because it will not be run otherwise, and the KEYBUK program *must* be placed also on this disk. The disk is then used by resetting the machine (ALT, CTRL, DEL keys together), and having the disk in Drive A: when requested to insert a system disk. The system will load, and you will see your word processor SHRDLU up and running. The usefulness of an AUTOEXEC.BAT file is that it avoids repetitive action. For example, you might always use your computer with a printer that you want to set into bold-face. This would be done by running a program, perhaps called PRINBOLD, each time you started work. By incorporating the line:

```
PRINBOLD
```

into your AUTOEXEC.BAT file, the PRINBOLD program would be run automatically. This assumes that you arranged things so that the printer was switched on along with the computer. If the printer is not switched on at the time when you run a printer control program, the actions of the program cannot be carried out. This makes it important to be able to include messages and pauses into any type of batch file, something that we'll look at shortly. Note that any AUTOEXEC file can be edited, and you can add to the file on your Master disk. Do not, however, make use of any AUTOEXEC file until you are sure that it is correct. A good way of testing is to rename the file as TEST.BAT, and try its effect out (by typing TEST) before using it in the AUTOEXEC.BAT form. For the use of CONFIG.SYS files, and the uses of FILES, BUFFERS and DEVICE in the AUTOEXEC.BAT file, see Chapter 6.

Batch subcommands

In a batch file, you can make use of any of the normal commands of MS-DOS, along with command options of the /A type, and filenames following commands. In addition you can use an extra set called the batch subcommands. These batch subcommands are not normally used outside a batch file and are listed here in alphabetical order.

NOTE that when batch commands carry out actions on text or other data files, these files must be present on the drive, or made available by way of an APPEND command (see Chapter 5). The PATH command affects only *program* files and has no effect on the availability of any data files.

ECHO

controls the screen display during the execution of a batch file. The simple straightforward use of ECHO is in the two forms ECHO ON and ECHO OFF. By using ECHO OFF, you will see a lot less appear on the screen while a batch file is executing, because no filenames will be displayed. This does not, however, turn off all screen display. The ECHO OFF command itself will be displayed on versions of MS-DOS prior to 3.3. For V.3.3 onward, it is possible to use:

ECHO OFF

which will suppress even this message. In addition, you would certainly not want to have error messages turned off, for example, and ECHO OFF does not do this. If, for example, your batch file contained the command DEL PIPPLE, and the file PIPPLE did not exist, then you would still see the message 'File not found' when the machine attempted to delete this file. Note, however, that this error does *not* cause the batch process to stop. Similarly, other messages that are produced while the DOS commands are being carried out are not hidden. A batch file will therefore normally start with ECHO OFF and ECHO ON might be used later only if there is some particular need to see what files are being executed. There is no need to use ECHO ON at the end of a batch file, because ECHO is automatically re-enabled at the start of each batch file.

There is one other use of ECHO, which is to display a message that is built into the batch file. Suppose that the batch file at one point starts a lengthy operation, such as comparing disks in two drives to check that they are identical. Whenever a computer starts something like this, it's a good idea to present a message on the screen to warn the operator that something is happening, will take some time, and should not be interrupted by pressing any keys. To present the message, you put into the batch file just before the start of the comparing action the command ECHO followed by a space and then the message, for example:

```
ECHO Please wait - comparing disks
```

– so that this message will appear on the screen and persist while the action is going on. This type of message cannot be suppressed by using ECHO OFF, and if you want it to be cleared off after the compare action is completed, you will need to make the command following the compare action a CLS, to clear the screen. A typical batch file of this type might be named CHECK.BAT and consist of the lines:

```
ECHO OFF
ECHO PLEASE WAIT...COMPARING
COMP %1 %2
ECHO ALL DONE
```

– which would require you to type the name of the batch file, followed by the names of the files to be compared, separated by spaces. You might, for example, type:

```
CHECK A:DIRFIL B:DIRFIL
```

– to check that two files on two different disks were identical. You would see the message ECHO OFF then the message about waiting, and then the comparison would be carried out. The message from the COMP program would be displayed, because such messages are not suppressed, so that you could tell whether the copies were identical or not. Don't be tempted to put a CLS into this type of program, because it would wipe the message before you had time to read it. If ECHO is used to print lengthy messages to the screen, it can be useful to be able to print blank lines so as to separate sets of instructions from each other. To do this, use:

```
ECHO.
```

with a full-stop following the word. This method of placing a blank line on screen using ECHO has been used by MS-DOS versions from 3.0 onwards, replacing an earlier method.

Example
```
ECHO Make sure that the data disk is in Drive
B:
ECHO and that it is not write-protected
ECHO
ECHO Now press any key to start
```

– will print the first two message lines, then a blank line and then the final message line.

REM

is an alternative to the use of ECHO, and is used for 'internal' messages. A REM command word in a batch file is followed by whatever message you want to deliver on the screen, just like the use of ECHO for messages. The important difference is that REM messages are suppressed if you use ECHO OFF, whereas ECHO text messages are not. The use of REM messages in batch files, along with ECHO OFF, allows you to leave reminders for yourself in the batch file, but prevents these messages from cluttering the screen.

For example, you might like to write a part of a batch file in the form:

```
REM DELETE ALL BAK FILES
DEL *.BAK
REM RENAME TXT TO NEW EXTENSION
RENAME *.TXT *.%1
```

– so that when you read the batch file (using TYPE or PRINT), you can see how it works at once without having to go through each command in detail. The alternative is to write the REM lines in the form:

```
REM DELETING BAK FILES
(Actions go here)
REM RENAMING TXT TO NEW EXTENSION
(Actions...)
```

– with no ECHO OFF at the start of the file, so that the REM lines appear as messages on the screen to remind you of what is going on, and are also present as reminders in the batch file when you TYPE it or PRINT it. Unless your batch files are very simple, it's important to put in REM lines as a reminder to yourself, because it is remarkably easy to forget exactly what a batch file does after a few months.

You will be glad of your REM lines when you find that there is some action that you would like to add to the file, or you want to change the file, or make a new copy as the basis of another batch file. A REM message can be up to 123 characters in length, but for neatness it is better to use REM lines of not more than 72 characters or so.

FOR..IN..DO

This set of instructions carries out a command or set of commands until a count has been completed. Very often, a batch file must repeat a set of commands until some condition is satisfied. The most common requirement is to carry out an action with each one of a set of different files. This could, of course, be done on an individual basis, using commands, or on a batch basis by putting the name of each file into the batch command. All of this is a waste of valuable human time, however, and it's much better done by the machine. The batch command that uses the words FOR, IN and DO is arranged to carry out just this type of repetition action on a group of files. The command consists of the words FOR..IN..DO, and the FOR is followed by 'variable name'. This consists of two percent signs followed by a letter, so that %%a, %%b, %%c and so on are all valid variable names. The point of this is that during the execution of the command, this quantity, the variable name, will take the name of each file in turn from a list or set of files that you provide as parameters in the batch file.

By using a variable name such as %%a, you can command actions on that file, such as DELETE

%%a, TYPE %%a, PRINT %%a and so on. This means that whatever action you have specified for %%a will be carried out on each file in the set in turn. Note carefully the difference between this and the use of %1, %2 and so on in the command to start a batch file. These are parameters that are passed into the batch file command by you when you type the name of the batch file and want to specify the filenames that it will work on. The %%a, %%b, %%c are *internal* parameters that are used to specify a filename from a list that is contained *inside* the batch file. Following FOR %%a, you need to specify the set of files that will be used, and whose names will be represented in sequence by %%a (or whatever letter you have used). This is done by typing IN, and then the set of filenames held within brackets. The set can be specified by using a wildcard, so that you can type IN (*.TXT) for all files using the .TXT extension, or you can specify a list of files, with the names separated by a space, such as:

IN(CHAP1.TXT CHAP5.TXT CHAP10.TXT)

If you have used a wildcard, such as:

IN(CHAP?.TXT)

then each file that corresponds will be represented in turn by %%a and whatever actions you have specified carried out. When the list is more selective, only these specified files will be used.

Finally, you need to specify what has to be done with each file, and this is whatever follows the word DO. If, for example, you used DO DEL %%a, then each file from the list would be deleted in turn, whereas if you used DO TYPE %%a, then each file would be displayed on the screen, and you would probably want to use the MORE filter (see Chapter 6) to ensure that the display was arranged in screen pages.

Example: the following batch file can be saved under the name REPEAT.BAT:
ECHO ON
FOR %%A IN (*.BAT) DO TYPE %%A

– which will show all of your BAT files on screen when you type REPEAT. By using ECHO ON, you can see the title of each file, rather than just a list of instructions. You need to use Ctrl-S to stop this list from scrolling, because the filters such as MORE, cannot be used in this type of command. This is unfortunate, but acceptable, because the use of Ctrl-S to stop the listing, and any other key to restart it, is quite easy. Another restriction is that the command that follows DO has to be a single command. You cannot list a set of commands to be carried out in sequence here, only a single command and any variable names that go with it, and all of the commands must be in a single line. This does not imply a single line on the screen or the printer, only that all of the commands must be complete before the RETURN key is pressed.

FOR is one command of MS-DOS batch files that can be used outside a batch file, but when this is done, the names for variables are preceded by one percent sign only.

Example

```
FOR %a IN (FIRST.TXT SECND.TXT THIRD.TXT) DO
DEL %a
```

– will delete a set of three specified files in a single MS-DOS command issued by typing this line and pressing RETURN.

IF..GOTO

Carries out a test and moves to another location in the batch file if the test has a TRUE result. A repetitive action can be even more useful if there is some method of testing whether or not you want the action carried out subject to some condition. The command words that are used in this way are IF and GOTO. The IF word is followed by a test, which can be one of three types, and depending on the result of the test (which will be TRUE or FALSE), then the program can either continue with whatever follows the IF part, or it can GOTO another part of the batch file. This part can skip some commands that follow the IF chapter, or it can return to an earlier part of the batch file, so that part of the file is repeated until the IF test is satisfied.

The point to which a GOTO refers is marked by a *label name*, a word of up to eight letters that follows a colon. This word will be used in a line of its own to mark where the label refers to, and will also be used following GOTO, but without the colon. You could, for example, use the word THERE as a label, as illustrated below, in a file called GOTEST.

```
ECHO OFF
IF NOT EXIST INX1 GOTO THERE
DEL INX1
:THERE
RENAME %1 INX1
```

– If the file INX1 exists, then the step DEL INX1 will be carried out. If this file does not exist, then the delete step is not executed because GOTO THERE makes the execution of the batch file move to the location THERE, and the colon signals that this is not a command, so that the following line is the next to be carried out. Since the program creates a file called INX1, you can run it both with the file not existing, and then with a file of that name existing, to see the difference (removing ECHO OFF will show the progress more clearly).

What you can do with this type of testing depends very much on what can be tested with IF. MS-DOS allows you to test three conditions. The most important, used in the example above, is to find if a file exists. The test

```
IF EXIST filename
```

will be TRUE if the file **filename** is in the current disk/directory, and whatever follows the IF test will be carried out. The filename could, of course, contain a different directory path or drive letter, but the file must be accessible if the TRUE result is to be obtained.

To test for a file not being on the disk, you can use

```
IF NOT EXIST filename
```

– which will allow the actions that follow this line to be carried out if the file is *not* present. This is the form of the test used in the previous example. Use of this type of test avoids the error messages that appear when you try to delete or rename a file that is not on the disk. Remember that you can specify a drive letter and path for files that would not appear on the disk in drive A. You can use the result of the IF test to deliver a message, and wait for you to insert the correct disk providing that this does not involve moving the batch file out of its drive.

Another item that can be tested by IF is the error number of a command that has just been executed. This will be 0 if the command has been executed without an error, but some other number, listed below, if there has been an error. Not all commands make use of error numbers. The test uses

ERRORLEVEL number

(*not* ERRORLEVEL=number), and the test will give a TRUE result if the ERRORLEVEL number that is returned is equal to or more than the tested number.

Commands that return ERRORLEVEL numbers are:

BACKUP	1	No files found to match specification
	3	Action terminated by using Ctrl-Break
	4	Error during BACKUP
FORMAT	3	User terminated with CTRL-Break.
	4	Serious error (faulty disk)
	5	Hard disk formatting abandoned.
GRAFTABL	1	Both old and new code pages installed
	2	No code pages are installed
	3	Parameter not valid
	4	DOS version earlier than 3.3 in use
KEYB	1	Faulty numbers or syntax
	2	No keyboard definition file
	3	Driver cannot be loaded
	4	Cannot find CON device
	5	Code page not ready
	6	Code page not in keyboard file
REPLACE	1	Error in command line.
	2	File(s) not found.
	3	Path to a file not found.
	5	File write protected.
	8	Insufficient memory to operate in.
	11	Parameters or number of parameters not valid
	15	Incorrect drive specified.
	22	Incorrect MS-DOS version
RESTORE	1	Files not on backup disk
	2	Sharing conflicts - some files not restored
	3	Esc or Ctrl-Break pressed
	4	Action ended by error
XCOPY	1	Files not found.
	2	User terminated wit CTRL-Break.
	4	Specification error (file, path

```
                     etc.).
            5 Disk error caused abort.
```

In each of these commands, an ERRORLEVEL number Ø means that the command was completed with no errors. This type of test allows you to test for some specified error, using a line such as:

```
IF ERRORLEVEL 2 GOTO MISTAKE.
```

This feature is rarely used for these commands, because these are actions that you seldom carry out in batch files. A very important point to note is the effect of the 'equal to or more than' type of test. When an ERRORLEVEL test line is written, it should test for the highest number that you expect. If you have a set of ERRORLEVEL lines in sequence, the numbers being tested for should be in descending order. This is illustrated in a following example.

A very common form of use of ERRORLEVEL depends on a short program which is not usually on the MS-DOS disk, but which can be found on various other disks, or as a public domain utility under various names. In one form it is called YN, and its action is to test for a key being pressed, and for that key being Y or N. If the key is Y, then the error-level number that is returned is Ø, otherwise the error-level number is 1.

Example
```
ECHO OFF
ECHO PRESS Y OR N
YN
IF ERRORLEVEL Ø ECHO THIS IS Ø
IF ERRORLEVEL 1 ECHO THIS IS 1
```

– This is recorded as TEST.BAT, and when it runs you are asked to press the Y or N key. The results are:

```
Y key pressed: Message THIS IS Ø
N key pressed: Message THIS IS Ø
                       THIS IS 1
```

– because when a 1 is returned this fulfils the IF ERRORLEVEL 0 condition by being more than 0, so that this message also is activated. This bears out the point about using tests in descending order of tested number. Note that the action of YN is such that any key other than Y will give the ERRORLEVEL number 1.

Example
```
ECHO OFF
CD C:WSTAR
WS
ECHO WANT TO SAVE TEXT TO A: ?
YN
IF ERRORLEVEL 1 GOTO GETOUT
COPY *.TXT A:
:GETOUT
CD C:
```

This selects a disk directory for WordStar and runs the program. At the end of using the program, the option is offered of backing up all the text to a disk in the A: drive. If the NO option is taken (any key except Y) then the COPY action is omitted and the root directory is selected again.

Another optional program, which is often found on MS-DOS distribution disk is CHOOSE. CHOOSE allows a set of numbers to be specified, and when CHOOSE runs only the pressing of one of these numbers (0 to 9) will allow the program to proceed. A message shows which number was chosen, and an ERRORLEVEL number is also returned which can be used in testing. The ERRORLEVEL number is the place number for the chosen item, so that using:

```
CHOOSE 12345
```

would give ERRORLEVEL numbers of 1 for choice 1, 2 for choice 2 and so on. If you used:

```
CHOOSE 2468
```

then choosing 2 would give ERRORLEVEL 1, choosing 4 would give ERRORLEVEL 2 and so on (choices 1,3,5,9 are invalid and have no effect).

Example
```
echo off
echo press number
choose 12345
if errorlevel 5 echo This is 5
if errorlevel 4 echo This is 4
if errorlevel 3 echo This is 3
if errorlevel 2 echo This is 2
if errorlevel 1 echo This is 1
```

– when this is run it will give the appropriate ERRORLEVEL numbers for a choice in the range 1 to 5 only. In this example, only ECHO lines have been used, but the principle is valid so that any command could follow the number in the ERRORLEVEL test. One common use is to implement a menu, using a different GOTO for each test line.

Other tests

You can also check if one piece of text (usually referred to as a 'string') is equal to another, using the double-equals sign (= =) as the symbol for comparison. This test can make use of filenames represented by parameters like %1 that you have typed, or filenames taken from a list and represented by variables like %%a. A more common use is to check the value of an 'environment parameter'. This is a form of name that you use and define for your own purposes. The value of these environment parameters is allocated by using SET, and such a name is enclosed in % signs, like %THISNAME%

Example
```
echo off
if "%tstnam%"=="setit" echo This is setit
```

– this will be ignored until you use a line:

```
SET tstnam = setit
```

after which the This is setit message will appear when the batch file is run. As before, what follows the test can be a command or a GOTO which will cause a different part of the batch file to be used. To reset the environment parameter, use the line:

```
SET tstnam=
```

(with nothing following the equality sign).

The SET action can be used along with the environment test within the same batch file. This can allow the use of loops that switch the values of environment variables, as the example shows.

Example
```
echo off
:one
if "%trynam%"=="on" goto two
if "%trynam%"=="off" goto three
goto end
:two
```

```
echo Trynam is ON
pause
set trynam=off
goto one
:three
echo Trynam is OFF
pause
set trynam=on
goto one
:end
```

This will have no effect until you run it following a
SET command, such as:

```
SET trynam=on or  SET trynam=off
```

but once trynam is assigned in this way, the batch
file switches between On and OFF each time you
press a key. To escape from this, you will have to
press Ctrl-C or Ctrl-Break.

On early versions of DOS, one batch file cannot
call another and return to the first file, because when
a second file is called, all records of the first one are
lost. There are various ways around this restriction,
some of them remarkably tortuous. Current versions
of DOS (3.3 onwards) allow the use of the CALL
instruction, allowing one batch file to call another in
the form:

```
ECHO OFF
REM Batch File 1
COPY %1 %2
CALL TWO
REM Starts up second file
COPY %3 %4
```

– in which the parameters %1 %2 %3 and %4 are used
in the file before and after calling the second file.
One of the simplest ways to implement this type of
action in versions prior to 3.3 is to use environment
variables to perform the calling and returning,
holding the name of the first batch file and a label
name within that file as a place to return to, and if
other values have to be taken from the second batch
file and returned to the first then this can be done;
alternatively other values that need to be preserved in
the first file can also be kept as environment
variables.

As an example, we can look at two simple batch
files, one of which calls the other, saves a name from

the second, and then returns. If a filename has been typed following the first batch file, its value can be preserved (it would normally be lost) after returning by holding this filename as an environment parameter. In the following example, create two files FIRST.BAT and SECOND.BAT and call the first one by using FIRST SECOND.BAT (or use any short test file that you have on the disk in place of SECOND.BAT).

Example

```
FIRST.BAT file
echo off
if not "%place%"=="" GOTO %place%
echo This is first
pause
set batret=%0
rem batret now equals first.bat
set place=nextstop
rem place to return to
set save=%1
rem save name following FIRST
second
rem call other file
:nextstop
type %save%
if "%show%"=="on" echo Show on
Echo This is nextstop
set place=
rem reset variable here

SECOND.BAT file
echo off
echo This is second
pause
set show=on
%batret%
rem go back to first, with show=on
```

The test for %place% in the second line of FIRST.BAT ensures that no attempt is made to go to a label that does not exist. If %place% has been assigned to *nextstop*, then %place% can be used as a label, just as if you had typed nextstop. The name of the first batch file is held as the variable batret and the name of the label to return to in this file is held as place, otherwise the return point would be the start of the first file again.

In this example, save is used to store the name of

a file that has been typed following FIRST, in order to show that this can be passed over intact. In the second file, an assignment is made to show to prove that this also can be returned. The use of the command second in the first file then calls the second batch file, and this does little else but assign show and return. On return, the various environment parameters are used to demonstrate that values have been passed.

Another method of passing control to another batch file and back again is to make use of a second copy of COMMAND.COM for running the second file. Under this system, there is no need to preserve parameters as environment variables, and the second program is called using:

```
COMMAND /C SECOND
```

– but this cannot pass variable values from the second batch file into the first.

PAUSE

The Pause command causes a message to appear on the screen and stops execution of the batch file until any key is pressed. The message is:

```
Press any key when ready...
```

but this can be added to by typing a message following PAUSE

Example
```
PAUSE Place data disk in Drive B:
```

– will, when this line executes, print the whole of this line (including PAUSE) and then the Press any key message. Note that the additional message does *not* appear if you have used ECHO OFF, so that a pause of this type is more likely to be configured as:

```
ECHO ON
PAUSE Place data disk in Drive B:
ECHO OFF
(Other commands)
```

– remember that the computer must still be able to read the batch file. If the Ctrl-Break or Ctrl-C keys are pressed during a pause you will be asked if you want to terminate the batch job, and pressing the Y key will terminate, any other key will cause the batch file to continue.

5 The external commands

The external commands of MS-DOS are really programs that run under MS-DOS and which have actions that are useful, they could just as easily be described as operating system utilities for MS-DOS. The reason for using the term 'commands' is that these programs extend the use of MS-DOS and are usually supplied along with the MS-DOS programs; having them separate avoids having to take up a lot of the memory of your computer with routines that you might not use very often, unlike the internal commands.

The external commands that are supplied on the distribution disk will vary according to the supplier of the disk, because when computer manufacturers supply the MS-DOS disk they are likely to include a few externals that are of particular use for that machine, or which the manufacturer thinks are generally useful. Do not be surprised if some of the external commands that are listed in this chapter are not on your own MS-DOS disk. Some of the programs that are described as external commands have dual uses, because they can also be used as *filters*, see Chapter 6. In addition, there are many programs available in the public domain which make excellent additional external commands for MS-DOS, and in the course of using MS-DOS you are likely to gather up many such programs.

Drive/directory

Since an external MS-DOS command is a program, the program has to be available when it is called, either with a disk in the current drive, or by having a PATH established to the directory where the program is stored. Users of twin-floppy machines can work with a copy of the MS-DOS disk permanently held in drive A:, and hard disk users can have an MS-DOS directory where all of the external command files and utility programs are stored, with a PATH to this directory established. Users of single disk machines, even the large-capacity 3.5" drives, are most likely to suffer from the problem of keeping these files in the correct place. The usual solution is to start an external command with the MS-DOS disk in the drive and to issue the external command in the form:

`command b:filename`

– where **command** is the name of the command, and **filename** is the name of any program on which it should act – if the action is to be on a disk, then this will be B:. You will then be prompted to change disks as required when the command is carried out.

Command line parameters

When the name of an external command is typed, this line of type is called the *command line*, and most command lines require one or more filenames (or other data items) to be typed following the command. These additional items are the command line *parameters* and if no parameters are supplied, or if the incorrect parameters are supplied, the external command will probably not run, and you will see an error message that draws your attention to the incorrect use of parameters. When these external commands are used in batch files, the filenames can be passed in the command line of the batch file, and picked up inside the file using the %1, %2 type of representation. Thus a batch file called using THISBAT File1 File2 can contain lines that use internal commands such as:

```
DEL %1
REN %2 %1
```

– taking the values of the parameters from the batch command line, and the same methods can be applied to those external commands that accept parameters on the command line.

Some external commands, like some of the internal commands, will accept optional 'modifiers' in the command line, and these are usually appended to a filename or similar parameter with a slash separating the parts of the command parameter. In some cases, several optional extras can be added, all separated by slashmarks. Some commands demand that the options are placed following any filename parameters, others demand that the options are placed immediately following the command word.

APPEND

The MS-DOS command APPEND does for data files what PATH does for program files, allowing the machine to search through different drives or directories for the data file that you want. Suppose, for example, that you have created three subdirectories called TEXT, SPSHEET and DBASE for keeping word processed text, spreadsheet data and database data respectively. You will have to specify the full path and name for data that you want to save, such as NEWBOOKchap1.txt, but with APPEND operating, you need not do so when you want to *read* data, since you can then specify a file name such as sheet1 and have all three subdirectories automatically searched for this file. The APPEND command uses the same syntax as the PATH command, with semicolons used to separate the different directories or drives.

Example
APPEND \TEXT;\SPSHEET;\DBASE

This example shows the three subdirectories as if they were one branch from root level, but of course you could specify items like WP\TEXT\LETTER or ABILITY\TEXT if you wanted to be more specific.

Like the PATH items, APPEND would normally be placed in a batch file that would be run before starting up a program that required the files to be searched. Another option to consider is that since the use of APPEND makes files available to any program that does not specifically request a path, these files are available to all programs. For example, if you specify that you want a file called B:needed or one called \DATA\LET\jones.let then these specific files will be obtained with no reference to the APPEND list, but if you simply ask for jones.let then the current drive/directory will be searched, followed by the list specified in the APPEND command.

APPEND, used alone, will produce a listing of the current APPEND paths in the order in which they were originally typed, which is the order in which files are searched.

APPEND, like PATH, can be revoked by using the form:

APPEND;

This means that you can have an overall set of PATH and APPEND commands in an AUTOEXEC.BAT file, but still alter the search path completely in the batch file for any program that requires something different. Note that the APPEND command, like PATH, may not be usable by some older types of programs which cannot make use of path names, but you can use SUBST (see later, this chapter) along with an 'imaginary' drive letter in order to bring such programs into the fold.

There are two options for Append, /X and /E. Using /X allows directory searches to be carried out from other directories, so that a DIR command need not specify a path if this path is used in an APPEND command. The APPEND/X must be placed before the main APPEND path in a batch file, and should be used only once in a session.

Example
```
APPEND/X
APPEND\TEXT
```

will allow a command such as DIR *.TXT to provide a directory of all files with that extension that exist in the TEXT directory. The /E option allows the APPEND path to be put in as an environment variable, using the form:

```
SET APPEND = C:\text
```

– which will have the same effect as the more usual syntax.

The use of the /X and /E options can cause problems when files are both read and written, as you may find that you can read from the correct directory but not write to it without specifying the directory explicitly – and not all programs permit this. In addition, any APPEND path should be cancelled before using BACKUP or RESTORE, and the APPEND path should appear in a batch file after an ASSIGN command (see later this chapter). Some manuals for MS-DOS that are packaged along with the computer make no mention of the options for APPEND because its use can in some cases cause more problems than it solves.

ASSIGN

ASSIGN allows you to 'blank off' a disk drive, so that any request for that drive is redirected to another drive. Suppose, for example, that you wanted to work with only your hard disk drive, redirecting anything intended for A: and B:. The form of the commands would be:

```
ASSIGN A=C B=C
```

with only the letters used, no colon following. After this pair of instructions has been implemented, a command such as:

```
A:prnset
```

will result in drive C: being searched for a program called *prnset*, and if you ask your word processor to save a file called B:text1.txt then this file will be saved on Drive C (in the root directory). In short, the use of the ASSIGN command has changed a two-floppy plus one hard disk computer into a hard disk only machine. The reassignment of a drive can be ended by using ASSIGN with the same letter on each side of the assignment (=) sign, and all assignments can be ended by using ASSIGN with no parameters.

Example
```
ASSIGN A=A
```

– will bring drive A back into service, and a similar command could be issued for Drive B.

Example
```
ASSIGN
```

– will end all assignments and return the normal use of the drives. The reassignment need not be confined to the real disk drives, because you can just as easily assign the RAM drive D: to any other drive, or, of course, a real drive to the RAM drive.

ASSIGN can also be used in a form such as:

```
ASSIGN C=A
```

to ensure that the hard disk will *not* be used, and this can be a simple precaution against unwanted interference with files on your hard disk when the computer is used to receive commands over the telephone lines. This assumes, of course, that a floppy disk would be adequate for such purposes.

ASSIGN was originally intended to allow the use of programs that were distributed on disks which were specified for Drive A to be used in a hard-disk system. The only function of ASSIGN now, for users of MS-DOS 3.0 onwards, is of reassigning the hard disk to a floppy as a way of protecting against intrusion. ASSIGN must *never* be used along with the following commands:

BACKUP RESTORE LABEL
JOIN   SUBST PRINT

ATTRIB

is a command that acts on a file or a set of files to
alter the read-only or archive settings. When a file is
saved, there is one byte allocated in the directory,
following the filename and extension bytes, for
attributes, meaning special features of the file. Six of
the eight bits of this byte are currently used as
follows:

Bit 0 Read-only
Bit 1 Hidden file
Bit 2 System file
Bit 3 Label used
Bit 4 Sub-directory file
Bit 5 Archive bit

These attributes are *on* if the bit is *1*, *off* if the bit
is *0*. The significance of *on* bits is:

Read-only	the file cannot be written to or appended to, and it cannot be deleted.
Hidden	the file is not seen in a normal directory listing.
System	the file is used by MS-DOS, and does not appear in a normal directory listing. This will usually be a *SYS* file.
Label used	applies to a disk root directory to show that a label name is present and should appear in the directory.
Sub-directory	shows that the file is part of a sub-directory and should not be listed in a normal directory search (APPEND can cancel this).
Archive	the file has been altered since the last time it was backed up (used by the BACKUP command, and also by other backup systems).

The ATTRIB command allows the read-only and the
attribute bits to be altered. The read-only attribute
uses code letter *R* and the archive attribute uses *A*

(MS-DOS versions from 3.2 onwards), with +
meaning *on* and − meaning *off*. These letter codes
are placed between the command word and the
filename, but if the command word is used without
a letter code, it will show if either of these two
attributes is *on* for a specified file. The filename can
include wildcards.

There is one option, ∕S which is useful when
ATTRIB is used with a wildcardfilename. When the
∕S follows the filename, any matching files in
subdirectories will be listed.

Example
ATTRIB BOOKTXT.TXT   produces on screen:
R A:\BOOKTXT.TXT

− meaning that this file is read-only, it cannot be
deleted or edited.

Example
ATTRIB +R C:\LURK\KEEPIT.DOC

− will make the file KEEPIT.DOC in this sub-
directory a read-only file.

Example
ATTRIB +R VAL*.*∕S

− will make any file whose name starts with VAL,
placed in any sub-directory, into a read-only file.

Example
ATTRIB -R *.*∕S

− will make any file on the disk which is read-only
into read-write, so that it can be deleted or edited.

Example
ATTRIB -A JUSBAK.OLD

− will remove the archive attribute from the file
JUSBAK.OLD so that commands (such as BACKUP
or XCOPY) will not make another backup copy of
this file.

BACKUP

MS-DOS has two commands that apply only to
machines that are fitted with a hard disk. These
commands are not present on the MS-DOS distribution disk for floppy-only machines. The first of these
is BACKUP which is used to transfer all files on a
hard disk to a set of floppy disks. BACKUP can be

used for a single file or for all the files on a hard disk, but there are more selective programs for backing up which are easier to use. The important feature of BACKUP (used on other forms of backup program as well) is that you are prompted to change floppy disks as and when necessary without having to take any decisions for yourself on when to do so. Before the BACKUP command is issued, you need to switch to a floppy drive and have a formatted data disk in that drive. The BACKUP command should be accessible on your hard disk by way of a suitable PATH statement.

The files that BACKUP produces are *not* in the same form as they are stored on the hard disk. In order to save space, the files are *archived*, compressed into a coded form that takes up considerably less storage space. Because of this coded form, you cannot read files that have been placed on to a floppy disk by BACKUP, and they can be restored to the hard disk only by using the complementary program, *RESTORE*.

BACKUP allows you a considerable choice about which files are backed up, such as filename, extension, date or time of creation or the archive bit (see ATTRIB). The floppy on which the backed-up files are stored will be cleared before use, so that care needs to be taken to check that no important files are held on the floppy. As each file is backed up, a notice will appear on the screen, and this can be redirected to the printer (see Chapter 6), or the screen print key can be used to make a note of the files. During the use of BACKUP, you will be prompted by a screen warning when a floppy disk needs to be changed. This will normally be required unless your hard disk is fairly empty or you have been very selective about which files are backed up. Normally, you would have copies of programs on their original floppy disks, so that backing up would be confined to data files only. If no form of file name or file selection is used, the whole content of the hard disk will be backed up, but this is a very unusual requirement.

Example
BACKUP C:\BIGFILE.TXT A:

– will back up a large file in the hard disk root directory on to floppy disks, using the A: drive. You will need to obey any messages that appear on the screen about changing floppy disks, removing each floppy disk in turn, labelling it, and putting on a write-protect tab. It is important to write a series number (1, 2, 3, ...) on each label in turn if more than one disk is needed. This is because the disks *must* be used in the same order when replacing data on to the hard disk.

Example
```
BACKUP C:*.*  A:
```

– will back up the entire hard disk. You will need to have sufficient floppy disks ready, formatted, and numbered in sequence.

Example
```
BACKUP C:\WPROC\BOOK*.TXT  A:
```

– will backup any file in this subdirectory that has the TXT extension. This is the most common way of using BACKUP with a wildcard, ensuring that only specified data files are backed up.

The options of BACKUP are /D, /F, /L, /M, /S, and /T.

The /D option letter is used following the floppy drive letter to specify files created or changed on or following a specified date. This date is typed following /D, separated by a colon.

Example
```
BACKUP C:\BOOKS\*.TXT  A:/D:01-02-89
```

– will backup any files with the TXT extension in the BOOKS sub-directory that were created or altered on or after 1st February 1989.

The /F option was introduced in V.3.3, and is placed following the floppy drive letter. This allows an unformatted disk to be used in the floppy drive when a BACKUP is performed, assuming that the FORMAT.COM program has been placed in a directory which is searched by the PATH command (see PATH).

Example
```
BACKUP C:\WPROC\*.*  A:/F
```

– will backup the files in the WPROC sub-directory onto unformatted floppy disks.

The /L option was also introduced with V.3.3, and allows a log file to be created using a specified drive and filename. If nothing is specified, the name of BACKUP.LOG is used and the file is placed in the root directory of the hard disk. The use of a log file obviated the need to make a note of the files that have been backed up, since the log file contains this list. The log file should *not* be put on drive A if the files are being backed up on this drive.

Example
```
BACKUP C:\WSTAR\*.TXT A:/L:B:LOGFIL.TXT
```

– will backup all files with the TXT extension in the WSTAR sub-directory and create a log list on drive B (assuming a machine with two floppy drives and a hard disk) using the filename of LOGFIL.TXT. It is more usual to put the log file on to the hard disk and then copy it to a floppy.

The /M option uses the archive attribute (see ATTRIB) to backup only these files which have been changed since BACKUP was previously used, so making it unnecessary to repeat the backing up of old files that have not been edited in any way.

Example
```
BACKUP   C:\WSTAR\*.TXT   A:/M
```

– will backup all files with the TXT extension that have been altered since the previous backup session. This form of BACKUP command can be placed, for example, in a batch file following the name of a data-handling program, so that altered files are automatically backed up when you leave the program.

The /S option ensures that when a directory is specified with no filenames then files that are placed in sub-directories of that directory will also be backed up.

Example
```
BACKUP C:\WRITE A:/S
```

– will backup any files in the WRITE directory and any files in sub-directories that lead off the WRITE directory.

The /T option allows you to specify a time, so that only these files which were created or modified after that specified time will be backed up. This is rarely necessary.

Example
```
BACKUP C:\WRD\*.TXT A:/T:13:00:00
```

– will backup only the files created in the afternoon, on or after 1.00 p.m.

Note: the BACKUP command will return an ERRORLEVEL number which can be used in a batch file, see Chapter 4.

CHKDSK

is a disk utility whose purpose is to check how a disk is used for storing files, and also to report any errors. Its use is more applicable to a hard disk, but it can be used equally easily for floppies.

When a disk, particularly a hard disk, has been used for some time, several files will have been deleted and others saved. It would be too much to expect a new file to fit in exactly the same space as a deleted one, so that the later files are likely to be spread over several parts of the disk, each part being a space that has been released by deleting an old file.

CHKDSK is used to report on how the storage space is allocated among directories, hidden files, normal files and free space, and it will also show, when it is applied to a file, how that file is split up for storage purposes. Optionally, CHKDSK will also attempt to mend disk faults that it finds, and will issue one or more of a large set of error messages if faults are found.

Note: because of the way that CHKDSK uses memory, it *must not* be used while the machine is running MicroSoft Windows, and will probably affect other forms of 'front-end' windowing programs.

Example
CHKDSK C:

– produced the display for a hard-disk.

```
Volume FILECARD created 5 Feb 1988 14:14
32610304 bytes total disk space
  110592 bytes in 6 hidden files
  165888 bytes in 71 directories
20834304 bytes in 1492 user files
11499520 bytes available on disk
  655360 bytes total memory
  179680 bytes free
```

This shows the analysis of files and directories, and also the memory analysis, something that can be useful. The comparatively small amount of memory shown as free reflects the use of the machine – the

CHKDSK program was run while WordStar 4.0 was also being run.

Example

```
CHKDSK C:\WSTAR\BOOKS\POCKTDOS\PDS1.TXT
```

– produced the display for this file:

```
Volume FILECARD created 5 Feb 1988 14:14
32610304 bytes total disk space
  110592 bytes in 6 hidden files
  165888 bytes in 71 directories
20873216 bytes in 1497 user files
11460608 bytes available on disk
  655360 bytes total memory
  179824 bytes free
C:\WSTAR\BOOKS\POCKTDOS\PDS1.TXT
Contains 5 non-contiguous blocks.
```

In this example, a filename has been specified as well as a disk drive and path, and the report ends with a note on the file, which contains 5 non-contiguous (not touching) blocks. This is an indication that the file has become very scattered in the course of editing, and that access to it will be slower.

Several utility programs exist which will re-organize a hard disk so that files can be brought together, and some of these program work in an intelligent way, giving priority to files in the root directory so that the fastest access is to these files, which should be your most important files like COMMAND.COM. The disk re-building routines of PC-Tools Plus are excellent in this respect. Some hard disk users re-build the disk layout weekly in order to keep running speeds fast, the less active user might use the technique once a month or twice a year. The re-building does not alter your use of the disk in any way, and no file is removed unless it has been damaged (and therefore cannot be used in any case). Remember, however, that this process can take a considerable time on a large hard disk – it's a matter of hours rather than minutes.

CHKDSK has two command line options:

/V will report on progress as the disk is being checked.

/F will repair damaged files as far as is possible.

Using the /F option means that the CHKDSK process can be slow, as any damaged files will be repaired. Sections of files which cannot be allocated anywhere are placed into files with names such as FILE1.CHK, FILE2.CHK and so on. These are useful only if they are text files, because program files cannot be put together again and run. You can use /F/V to make both the mending and the reporting actions run together. Note that the /F option does *not* make a scattered file into a unified file, it closes open files and tries to reallocate fragments and has no action on correctly closed files, no matter how scattered they are.

Note: messages of CHKDSK make reference to disk organization, such as referring to *clusters* (groups of sectors). You do not need to know in detail what these names refer to, but any numbers that appear should be noted in case you need to use them in conjunction with another program for file recovery.

The report messages are:

Contains n non-contiguous blocks – indicates that the file is scattered. If most of your files return this message, the disk needs to be re-organised.
Convert directory to file (Y/N)? – means that the directory whose name is shown is no longer usable, and you have the option of converting it to an ordinary file format, which would allow you to use file-recovery utilities to extract data from the file.
Convert lost chains to files (Y/N) – a file fragment has been found. Answer Y if this is a text (ASCII) file, N otherwise.
n bytes disk space freed – a file has been shortened releasing space on the disk.
n lost clusters found in m chains – you have the option of converting these unattached fragments into a file, or delete them.

The standard error messages are:

Allocation error, size adjusted– error in allocation of disk sectors, which the /F option can repair.
Corrections will not be written to disk– errors found, not repaired. Try again with the /F option.
Entry has a bad attribute/link/size– directory fault found.
Errors found, F parameter not specified

– Errors can be corrected by using CHKDSK again with /F option.

`Has invalid cluster, file truncated–` Damaged file found and closed. Can be used only if a text file. If this was a program file, delete it immediately, **do not attempt to use it.**

`Probable non-DOS disk. Continue (Y/N)? –` Disk unformatted or formatted by a different type of machine.

`Tree cannot be processed beyond this point –` error in subdirectory branching from the named directory.

`Disk error writing FAT1 or FAT2 –` File allocation table on disk can be corrected. Two such tables exist, and the number is shown. You will have to use a disk utility (PC-Tools Plus, Ultra, Nortons) to correct the FAT.

`Crosslinked on cluster n –` a cluster is allocated to two files. Copy each file to another disk, and then salvage.

`Insufficient room in root directory –` you are converting fragments into files, and have run out of disk space. Copy complete files to another disk, delete from the faulty disk, and use CHKDSK again.

`Invalid subdirectory –` incorrect entry in a subdirectory, which might be repairable if the /F option is used.

Example
`CHKDSK C:\WP\TEXT\*.TXT/F/V`

– checks the disk and all files with the TXT extension, looking for errors, reporting them and attempting to mend damaged files.

COMMAND

starts up another processor program for commands, normally another copy of COMMAND.COM. This is used in order to allow a program, the *parent* program to be left temporarily, but retained in memory while another program, the *child* program is run. Since this second program is run using a second copy of COMMAND.COM, there should be no conflicts with the parent program. The second copy of COMMAND.COM is released by typing EXIT (press RETURN).

Example

COMMAND

– loads in the second copy of COMMAND.COM, which will be released when EXIT is typed.

There are three option letters, /C, /E, and /P. The /C option allows a command to be executed by the second COMMAND.COM as soon as it is loaded.

Example

COMMAND /C TYPE NOTE.TXT

– will load the second copy of COMMAND.COM and perform a TYPE action on the specified file. Use EXIT to return to the original task.

The /E option allows the allocation of memory for environment variables (see SET) to be changed, using a number 160 to 32768 bytes (V.3.2 on), which should be a multiple of 16. V.3.1 uses numbers 10 to 2048, referring to 16-byte *paragraphs*.

Example

COMMAND /E:1024

– will load in the second copy of COMMAND.COM and make a space of 1024 bytes (1K) for environment variables. The environment variables from the parent program can still be used. The /P option is used when the second copy of COMMAND.COM is to be used even after EXIT is typed. This may be necessary if the /E option is used to change the size of the environment. The /P option will be ignored if the /C option has been used.

COMP

is used to compare disk files that ought to be identical. The files can be compared line by line or character by character. The command word can be followed immediately by its option letters, separated by slashmarks, then by the filenames. The options are used to vary the type of reports and detection methods. When COMP is used to compare text files, the default method is line by line, so that differences between lines will be reported in the form of the lines rather than the differences in characters. By using the /B option, comparison of text files can be made on a character basis, so that any character that is different will be reported. When COMP is used to compare program files (extensions EXE, COM, SYS, OBJ, LIB, BIN) the comparison is *always* character by character, unless this is over-ridden by the /L option. The standard method of reporting text files will print the whole area of difference. After a difference has been found, COMP will continue only after finding that the next two lines in one file match the next two lines in the other file – this 'resynchronize' number can be changed by an option and the standard options are:

/A show differences by using ... rather than full lines
/C treat all letters as upper-case so that differences due to case are not reported
/L force line comparison for EXE, COM, SYS, OBJ, BIN files
/LB200 use 200 line buffer, default is 100
/N add line numbers to locate differences
/T leave tab characters rather than counting to spaces
/W ignore spaces at start and end of line, count tabs and multiple spaces as a single space each
/3 start comparing again after 3 sets of lines are found to be identical (default is 2)

The files that will be used in the following examples are:

CHK1.DOC consisting of:
```
Linematch
This is the first line
and this is the Second
This is the third in CHK1
and this is CHK1 fourth
with this as fifth
This is the sixth
and this is the seventh
```

and CHK2.DOC consisting of

```
Linematch
This is the first line
and this is the second
with this as fifth
This is the sixth
and this is the seventh
```

Example
COMP CHK1.DOC CHK2.DOC   gives:

```
***** c:chk1.doc
This is the first line
and this is the Second
This is the third in CHK1
and this is CHK1 fourth
with this as fifth
***** c:chk2.doc
This is the first line
and this is the second
with this as fifth
*****
```

Example
```
COMP/A/C CHK1.DOC CHK2.DOC          gives:
```
```
*****                          C:chk1.doc
and this is the Second

...
with this as fifth
***** C:chk2.doc
and this is the second
with this as fifth
```

and in this comparison, the intermediate differing
lines are represented by the dots. Note that the lines
and this is the second are regarded as identical
because second and Second are considered identical
when the /C option is used.

Example
```
COMP/C/N CHK1.DOC CHK2.DOC          gives:
```
```
***** C:chk1.doc
3: and this is the Second
4: This is the third in CHK1
5: and this is CHK1 fourth
6: with this as fifth
***** c:chk2.doc
3: and this is the second
4: with this as fifth
```

Example
```
COMP/B CHK1.DOC CHK2.DOC        gives (part only):
```
```
00000033: 53 73
0000003B: 54 77
0000003C: 68 69
0000003D: 69 74
0000003E: 73 68
00000040: 69 74
fc: c:chk1.doc longer than c:chk2.doc
```

– in which only a part of the long print out has been shown. This shows the position in the file (in terms of hexadecimal numbers) for each mis-match, so that this type of comparison is suited only to program files – it is one useful way to detect a virus if a file known to be uninfected is available.

Note: Line-by-line comparisons make use of a memory buffer of 100 lines when unmatched lines are found. Comparing two texts that contain a large number of consecutive differences can overflow this buffer, giving the message:

`Resynch failed. Files are too different`

The comparison can be tried again, using the LB option in the form /LB250 which permits a 250 line buffer. The LB option letters must be followed by a suitable number.

The / T option (don't expand tab character to spaces) allows the tab character to be compared rather than the default of the spaces that it would cause in a file (up to 8). The / W option allows excessive spaces to be ignored, so that a comparison does not report a difference merely because one file has a difference in spacing.

Other error messages are:

`Cannot open filename`– incorrect specification of a file or drive.
`Out of memory`– not enough memory to store the files.

DISKCOMP

is intended for floppy disk users only, and should not be applied to a hard disk, nor to RAMdisk nor to networks. It allows two floppy disks to be compared, noting any differences. The options, seldom used, are:

/1 – compare Side 1 of each disk only
/8 – compare only first 8 sectors of each track
DISKCOMP must not be used if ASSIGN, JOIN or SUBST have been previously used and not cancelled.

Example
`DISKCOMP A: B:`

– will compare disks in the two floppy drives, assuming that DISKCOMP is on the A: drive disk (or on a hard disk if a hard-disk card is fitted, or in the RAMdrive).

Example
DISKCOMP A: B:/1/8

– compares Side 1 and first 8 sectors per track only.

Example
DISKCOMP

– will compare disks that are inserted one after the other in the A: drive. You are prompted as to when to insert disks, labelled as first and second.

Error messages are:
Compare error on side x, track y – shows where error exists so that a disk utility program can be used to locate this track.
FIRST diskette bad or incompatible – incorrect formatting of the first disk. Run CHKDSK on this disk before proceeding.
SECOND diskette bad or incompatible – the formatting of the second disk is incorrect. Try CHKDSK on this one before attempting to use DISKCOMP again.

DISKCOPY

used for floppy disks to make a complete copy of one disk to another. The destination disk should preferably be formatted and unused, but if it contains files, these will be over-written. If it has not been formatted, then formatting will be carried out before copying – but this takes longer. The source disk from which files are to be copied should *always* be write-protected before starting to use DISKCOPY, particularly if a single floppy drive is being used.

The important point about DISKCOPY is that it copies byte-by-byte with no regard for files, so that system tracks, hidden files, deleted files, corrupted files etc. will all be copied across to the destination disk. Always use DISKCOPY if you want to make an exact copy of a disk which contains files you want to work on with a disk utility program (if, for example, you want to 'undelete' files).

If DISKCOPY is used on a machine with a single floppy drive, you will be prompted to change disks when necessary.

Example
DISKCOPY A: B:

– copies the entire contents of the disk in drive A to the disk in drive B. If this is used with a single drive you will be prompted to change disks.

Example
DISKCOPY A:

– uses single drive only, and prompts you to change between source and destination disks as required.

Messages:
Formatting while copying – destination disk was unformatted.
Copy another diskette (Y/N)? – another copy.
Copy not complete – source disk probably copy-protected or corrupted.
Disks must be the same size – destination disk has incorrect format.
Target diskette is write protected – remove write-protect tab.

EXE2BIN

is for the use of machine-code programmers only. The command word is followed by the name of an EXE file, and the action is to convert this into a COM file *if* this is possible. You are only likely to know if this is possible if you have written the EXE program for yourself, or have detailed information on it. The essential features of such a file are:

1 It must take up no more than 64K along with its data and stack.
2 It must not refer to other segments.

The advantage of converting from EXE to COM is that COM files load faster and take up less space in the memory.

FASTOPEN

allows fast access to any file that has been used during a session, by temporarily storing the location that the file occupies on the disk into the memory of the computer. This can be used only with a hard disk system, and does not apply to networks, floppies nor RAMdisk. It is particularly advantageous if you do not use a cache memory for this purpose. The number of files can be specified, each needing 35 bytes of memory. If no number (10 to 999) is specified, 34 files will have their details stored.

FASTOPEN should be included in the AUTOEXEC.BAT file, since it ought to be used only once in a session, and should be used before any work is done. You must not use FASTOPEN if you also use ASSIGN, JOIN or SUBST.

Example
FASTOPEN C:50

– will start the use of FASTOPEN, with up to 50 files having their details held in memory.

FDISK

is used to prepare a hard disk for formatting, in particular the hard disk that is supplied as a built-in disk. Many hard disk systems can be obtained as cards that fit internally, and allow the use of both floppy drives on a twin-floppy machine (allowing the use of both 5.25" and 3.5" floppy drives along with a hard disk). These 'hard-card' systems usually come with suitable software of their own for installing and formatting the disk, so that FDISK is not needed.

FDISK, like FORMAT, must *never* be held on the hard disk in case it is re-used by accident. This is a particular hazard if you use friendly 'front-end' programs that allow you to run files that are pointed at by the mouse, because a small displacement of the hand when the mouse button is pressed can lead to running the wrong file.

FDISK makes considerable reference to *partitions*. MS-DOS versions prior to 4.0 could cope with 32 Mb disk sizes, and if the disk were physically larger than this, it had to be divided into sections, each of 32Mb or less, and each with a different logical drive letter. If the hard disk is of 32 Mb or less, the FDISK program will by default use only the single drive letter C:, but you have the option in FDISK of partitioning even this disk into more than one drive letter.

Since FDISK is normally used only once in the history of a computer, its use should be fully described in the manual for that computer. If an add-on disk is bought, then it is likely to use different software, or will also describe FDISK in detail. After a partition is installed (and this must be done even if the disk size is less than 32Mb, using one partition only), you need to use another option of FDISK to make the partition active. Once this has been done, you can leave FDISK and use FORMAT to format the disk ready for use. For a large disk size, formatting can take a considerable time, measured in hours rather than minutes for a disk of more than 32Mb.

FIND

is a text file utility that allows each place where a set of characters (a string) has been used to be found in a file, a keyboard input, or when used as a filter the output of a program. These last two options are valuable features which are seldom used. For filter use of FIND see Chapter 6.

Option letters, used between FIND and filename:
/C display line number(s) where the string was found
/N number the lines to show position in file
/V display all lines *except* these containing the string

The string to be found must be enclosed in quotes ("), and if the string contains quotes, double quotes must be used. Care is needed about small words or letter groups – if you specify "a" you will get each line that contains the letter in a word, but if you specify " a ", with spaces, then only the letter used by itself will count.

Example
```
FIND "computer" C:\text\oldbook\chap1.txt
```

– will find each place where the word *computer* occurs in the selected file.

Example
```
FIND " the "
```

– will find when you type the word the, and note this by repeating the line on screen. Type Ctrl-C or Ctrl-Break to end the search.

Example
```
FIND/N "third" C:CHK1.DOC
```

produces on screen (on my system)

```
---------- C:chk1.doc
[4]This is the third in CHK1
```

For examples of FIND used as a filter, see Chapter 6.

FORMAT

prepares a floppy disk for use, or wipes a previously used disk clean. This is one of the few commands that can totally delete data beyond hope of recovery. It can be used for a hard disk, and though it will not necessarily destroy all of the data beyond recovery (depending on the disk partitioning), hard disk users should ensure that FORMAT is not present on the disk.

There are many options, several of which are of little interest except to users of odd disk formats. When FORMAT is used from a floppy disk, the disk containing FORMAT should be write-protected.

Example
FORMAT B:

– with the disk containing the FORMAT program in the A: drive, this will format another disk whether you have a single drive or a twin drive. For a twin floppy drive you will be prompted to put the disk to be formatted into drive B:, for a single drive you will be prompted to change disks.

The options, in order of usefulness are:

/S – put system tracks on to the disk while format-ting. This *must be the last option* if several options are specified.
/V – prompt for 11-character label name after formatting.
/B – format with 8 sectors per track and leave space for system tracks to be added later. See SYS command.
/T:80 – format with 80 tracks (if disk drive permits). This can be used to format a 3.5" 720K disk on a 1.44Mb drive.
/N:8 – format with 8 sectors per track (instead of 9). N is usually used along with T for an unusual format.
/8 – format with 8 sectors per track.
/1 – format as a single-sided disk.

Restriction: FORMAT must not be used on any drive that has been the subject of ASSIGN, JOIN or SUBST commands.

Example
FORMAT B:/S

– formats a disk with system tracks to use as a self-starting disk.

Example
FORMAT A:/V

– will carry out the formatting as usual, and then prompt for a label of up to 11 characters.

Example
FORMAT B:/B

– will format a disk with 8 sectors per track and with system tracks left vacant so that they can be added later using the *SYS* command.

Example
FORMAT C:

– will format a hard disk which has been partitioned by using FDISK previously.

FORMAT returns ERRORLEVEL codes which can be used in batch files, see Chapter 4.

GRAPHTABL

is a utility for users of the CGA video board (this includes the older Amstrad machines, and the Sinclair PC 2000) which normally cannot display the ASCII codes 128 to 255 when the screen is operating in graphics mode. Using GRAPHTABL allows these characters to be displayed. The program is used by some applications programs, notably the all-in-one office program *Ability* to allow characters to be shown on the screen in graphics mode as a way of implementing a word-processor which can display underlining and other effects.

The usual method of using GRAPHTABL is by using the command in the AUTOEXEC.BAT file, if the program is required, or in the batch file that calls a program that requires the use of GRAPHTABL. Versions of MS-DOS from 3.3 onwards have an extended version of GRAPHTABL which allows a code page to be selected from which characters are drawn. This latter version of GRAPHTABL also returns ERRORLEVEL numbers for use in a batch file.

GRAPHICS

is used along with suitable printers to print the graphics screens. If the printer is an IBM-compatible colour printer, the prints can be in colour. GRAPHICS is used for graphics screens (such as are used to display drawing or painting programs) and is not used for text screens (even when the text appears in boxes). The use of GRAPHICS allows the (SHIFT) PrtSc key to be used in printing graphics screens, as it can be used ordinarily for printing text screens.

If your printer is not IBM compatible for such screens, you will need to run one of the many available conversion programs, such as PRTSCFX, which is available from Shareware and public-domain software suppliers. The standard printing method for monochrome printers is to print dark lines on a white background. High resolution screens are printed sideways.

There are many options, not all of which may be available on some versions. The general ones are:

/R – reverse shading to print white lines on black background (useful when you use Microsoft Windows)

/F – turn the printed version through 90°

/C – centre the print on the paper

/B – (IBM Color Printer only) prints the background colour of the screen as well as the foreground colours.

/LCD – prints graphics as they appear on the LCD screen of a portable computer.

The other options concern the type of printer that is to be used. If none of these options is specified (or if *GRAPHICS* is used) then the IBM PC Graphics Printer is assumed, or a compatible printer.

COLOR1 – use IBM PC Color Printer with black ribbon

COLOR4 – use IBM PC Color Printer with red/green/blue ribbon

COLOR8 – use IBM PC Color Printer with cyan/magenta/yellow/black ribbon

COMPACT – use IBM PC Compact Printer

COLORJET – use IBM Color Jet Printer.

If you intend to make use of GRAPHICS, with or without PRTSCFX, then the program should be on the start-up disk, and its name should be in the

AUTOEXEC.BAT file. Note that GRAPHICS allocates memory for storing images, and this memory cannot be re-used for anything else unless you reboot and do not run GRAPHICS this time.

Example
GRAPHICS/R

- loads in the GRAPHICS program with black and white correctly shown on the printout. This is useful if the screen image uses a white background, because this will normally print as black, using a lot of printer time.

Example
GRAPHICS COLORJET/B

- print graphics screen with IBM colour inkjet printer and with background colour printed.

JOIN

is one of the utilities that has to be used with considerable care, because some other utilities cannot be used along with it. Its effect is to make a drive appear to be part of a directory, so extending the use of the directory. The directory must be directly off the root and must be empty. The form of the command is JOIN drive directory-path. The original drive letter cannot be used in its normal way after joining.

Example
JOIN A: C:DRIVE_A

which will have the effect of allowing you to use the subdirectory DRIVE_A on the hard disk C: as if it contained everything that is physically present on the disk in drive A. If your disk in Drive A: contained a set of programs and data files arranged in subdirectories, then you will find this structure in Drive C: now by typing CD\DRIVE_A.

The disk in Drive A: can now be used only by way of the directory DRIVE_A, not by using A:, so that error messages will appear if a PATH command includes A:.

Example
JOIN B: A:DRB

- makes the disk in the B: drive behave as if it were the directory DRB of the A: drive.

A join can be broken by using another JOIN command that specifies the original letter followed by /D .

Example
JOIN A:/D

– will break the use of drive A as a sub-directory, assuming that the JOIN.EXE program is on a path that can be reached (it must *not* be on the A: drive in this example.

JOIN by itself will display whatever joining actions are currently in effect. As usual, this requires that the JOIN.EXE program is in the path that is searched for program files.

JOIN must *not* be used:
– on a network
– along with ASSIGN or SUBST
– when the commands BACKUP, DISKCOMP, DISKCOPY, FORMAT or RESTORE will be used.

KEYB

is the keyboard driver program that is supplied with V.3.3 onwards, differing from the earlier version of which the UK version is KEYBUK. The KEYB command can use the same pair of letters to denote country, but can in addition be followed by a *code page* for the particular character set. Another option allows the path to a keyboard file to be typed. This is necessary because the older version used files such as KEYBUK.COM, which could be searched for by a PATH line in the AUTOEXEC.BAT file, but the newer KEYB uses data files, and this syntax avoids the need to have to use ASSIGN for searching.

Example
KEYB UK

– will select the UK version of the key layout.

Example
KEYB CF,863

– will select the Canadian French keyboard layout, using Code page 863 for its characters.

Example
KEYB GR,437,C:\MSDOSkey.sys

– selects the Greek keyboard layout, using Code

page 437 and specifying that the keyboard driver file is on the \MSDOS\ path.

KEYBXX

uses the XX for two letters that denote country, such as UK, FR, US etc. This is the older version (before the use of Code pages in V.3.3) for setting the keyboard for use with a specific country. The normal method of using KEYBXX is in the AUTOEXEC.BAT file in the form:

KEYBUK

– assuming that the file KEYBUK.COM is present in the drive or on a path that can be searched.

LABEL

allows a name of up to 11 characters to be put into the disk directory as a volume name or label. The LABEL name will appear each time the directory for the disk is printed, as the VOLUME name.

The name can include spaces, though the characters * ? / \ ¦ . , ; : + = < > [ ] are *not* allowed. If you have a labelled floppy disk in a drive that has been affected by ASSIGN or JOIN then the label will not appear on a directory listing.

LABEL, used along or with only a drive specified, allows a label name to be entered, or an existing name to be deleted. If the RETURN key is pressed when the label name is called for, any existing name can be deleted with the following option. The alternative method is to type the new label name following the LABEL command.

LABEL should not be used when ASSIGN or SUBST have been used.

Example

LABEL B:

– will produce a prompt for a new label name. This can be typed, then RETURN pressed, or RETURN can be pressed by itself. You are then asked:

Delete current volume label (Y/N)?

– which allows you to delete an existing label, or even the one you have just entered.

Example
LABEL A: ACCOUNTS

– will label this disk as ACCOUNTS when the directory is displayed.

MODE

is a multi-purpose command for altering the use of the screen and printer outputs. It can set the screen output to 40 or 80 characters per line, and to colour or monochrome (assuming the screen *can* be switched). A parallel printer can be set to print 80 or 132 characters per line and 6 or 8 lines per inch, assuming that the printer is capable of such settings. A serial output can have its serial protocols of baud rate, parity, number of data bits and number of stop bits set so as to suit a serial printer. Output to the parallel port can be re-directed to the serial port as a way of printer-switching. The letters that follow the MODE command decide which peripheral will be affected, and the codes which are used are listed below.

LPT1: Parallel printer
COM1: Serial output
40, 80, C040 or C080 : Screen character/colour options

Starting with V.3.3, MODE can also be used for preparing, activating, displaying and restoring code pages for use with some IBM printers and some types of screen displays. For parallel printer control, MODE will use the port name, usually LPT1, followed by the number of columns per line and the number of lines per inch, with the *P* option used to prevent time-out messages being printed if the printer is slow. This applies also if the printer incorporates a buffer of its own which means that there will be a comparatively long interval between successive calls for characters for the printer. A daisywheel printer will almost always require the use of the *P* option, though if the printer is driven by a word-processor, the action may be built in to the word-processor.

Example
MODE LPT1: 132,8

– sets the parallel printer to 132 characters per line, 8 lines per inch. The default is 80 characters per line,

6 lines per inch. To set only the number of lines per inch, omit the first figure but keep the comma.

Example
MODE LPT1:,8

– sets 8 lines per inch, leaving characters per inch setting unchanged.

Example
MODE LPT1:,,P

– will make it easier to send text continuously to a slow printer such as a daisywheel type. This can be done in the AUTOEXEC.BAT file.

Serial port control

This is specified by using COM1 or COM2 (one of these may already be used by an internal modem); DOS versions 3.3 onwards allow the use of COM3 and COM4 if they are fitted. The COM specifier will be followed by figures for:

- Baud rate, using 110, 150, 300, 600, 1200, 2400, 4800, 9600 and (for 3.3 on) 19200.
- Parity, which is N (none), 0 (odd) or E (even).
- Databits, the number of bits per word, 7 or 8.
- Stopbits, the number of stop bits, 1 or 2
- and also the *P* specifier to prevent time-out signals

The default settings are even parity, 7 data bits and 1 stop bit (2 if 100 baud is selected). The existing setting will be used if in a MODE command there is nothing placed between the commas – there must always be four commas present.

Example
MODE COM1:1200,N,8,1

– sets up to use the serial port with 1200 baud, no parity, 8 data bits, 1 stop bit. This is a very common combination of settings for modem use.

Example
MODE LPT1:600,,,1,P

– changes baud rate to 600, makes no change to parity or number of data bits, uses one stop bit and will send to a slow printer (as for parallel printer).

Screen settings

Note that not all computers will accept some of these settings, since their usefulness depends on the type of graphics card that is fitted.

MODE 40	40 characters per line, which is useful for large-print displays on screen.
MODE 80	the default 80 characters per line.
MODE BW40	40 characters per line monochrome
MODE BW80	80 characters per line monochrome
MODE CO40	40 characters per line colour
MODE CO80	80 characters per line colour

MODE as applied to the screen can also be used to test and adjust the centring of text. Used in the form MODE, with L or R, the screen text can be moves left or right. This is seldom useful without the addition option T which will allow a test of the screen centring to be made at the same time.

Example
```
MODE,R,T
```
produces on screen:

```
01234567890123456789012345678901234567 8
901234567890123456789012345678901234567 89
Do you see the leftmost 0? (Y/N)
```

– and you can press Y if this character is visible, N if not. This can be followed by using MODE,L,T to test for the right-most character.

Redirection of a printer

This works in one direction only – the redirection of a print output from the default parallel port to the serial port, or the cancellation of this redirection.

Example
```
MODE LPT1:=COM1:
```

– makes all output that is normally sent to the parallel printer go to the serial port instead. Note that there must be no spaces either side of the = sign.

Example
```
MODE LPT1:
```

– restores the parallel port. Use MODE LPT1:,,P if the output is to a *slow* printer.

MODE used with code pages

Starting with V.3.3, MODE can also be used along with code pages, a system which is explained in more detail in Chapter 6. For that reason, only an outline of the use of MODE for code pages will be given here. The files DISPLAY.SYS and PRINTER.SYS must have been used in the CONFIG.SYS file.

MODE can be used to prepare code pages for use from the CPI files that are present on the MS-DOS distribution disk. The MODE command should specify CON or PRN, and the information files will also be specific to the devices. The files supplied with V.3.3 are:

4201.CPI	for IBM Proprinter 4201 (several other printers, such as the Canon bubblejet, emulate this printer)
5202.CPI	for IBM Quietwriter III and emulations
EGA.CPI	for EGA video board
LCD.CPI	for LCD screens on portable computers.

Example
```
MODE CON CODEPAGE PREPARE=((850,860)
C:MSDOSEGA.CPI)
```

– will prepare codepage files for the EGA screen and pages 850 and 860.

Example
```
MODE PRN CODEPAGE SELECT=850
```

– selects the use of codepage 850 for the printer, assuming that a suitable CODEPAGE PREPARE line has been used.

Example
```
MODE CON CODEPAGE /STATUS
```

– will print out the currently used codepage for the screen, along with the numbers of other codepages that have been prepared.

Example
```
MODE PRN CODEPAGE REFRESH
```

– will renew the use of codepages on a printer that has been turned off at some time and which is no longer responding to code page information after being turned on again.

MORE

is used only as a filter in conjunction with the output of other programs. See Chapter 6.

NLSFUNC

is another of the code-page utilities which is seldom required. Normally, the information that is specific to a country such as currency sign and whether it is placed before or following a number, the time format and the date form, are all contained in the file that appears in the COUNTRY command (see earlier, this chapter). If a different file is to be used, then NLSFUNC can be followed by a path and filename. If the COUNTRY file is to be used, NLSFUNC must be run first. Both NLSFUNC and COUNTRY should be used in the AUTOEXEC.BAT file, or in a separate batch file if these changes have to be made for the use of one particular program (the word-processor that you use to write to customers in Greece, for example).

Example
NLSFUNC

– sets up ready for the use of COUNTRY

Example

NLSFUNC C:\MSDOS\FOREIGN.SYS

PRINT

is a command whose effect is to print an ASCII file of text on the printer. When you use PRINT, followed by the name of a file, the file will be printed on paper, but the computer can still be used for other tasks. PRINT is a time-sharing action, one that is done by loading in text in batches from the disk, storing the text in memory, and sending the text to the printer in any spare time that the computer happens to have.

You cannot, of course, remove the floppy disk from which the computer is reading the text, or alter the directory if you are working from a hard disk but you can load in a program from another drive or run such a program while the printing is being carried out. A hard disk user would normally use CD to get to the directory where the files for printing were stored, and have a suitable PATH set up to the PRINT command. Once printing has started, other programs can be run provided that this does not involve another CD command to leave the current directory. You cannot, however, carry out any other printing action until the printer is free for use again. The action of PRINT can set up a queue of files to be printed, and unless you terminate the action in some way, you cannot use the printer for any other printing actions.

When you make use of the PRINT command for the first time in a computing session, you might want to change some of the settings. These settings can be changed by issuing command letters in the first PRINT command, but at the first use of PRINT, you can also make one alteration without any special effort. This option is of the name of the device to which print characters will be sent, and the option takes the form of the question:

Name of list device [PRN]

You then press RETURN unless you are using a serial printer, in which case you can type COM1: and then press RETURN. Obviously, the printer must be connected and switched on, with continuous paper ready.

When printing starts, the normal prompt, such as C>, will return to show that printing is being done in the background, and that you can use the machine for other purposes. There are six other options that can also be made at the time of the first use of PRINT. This can be done at the same time as you specify a list of files to be printed, or you can type PRINT by itself followed by these selections, as follows:

/ B:1024 sets the print buffer store to 1024 characters. The larger the number here, the easier it is to interleave the printing action with any other computing. Use numbers that are multiples of 512 preferably. The default is 512.

/Q:12 allows you to use a queue of up to 12 files waiting to be printed. The default is 10.

/S:5 means that the computer will spend one sixth of its time in printing, using a ratio of computing to printing of 5:1. The default is 8. It is not always possible to predict what effect this will have on the rate of printing, because if the printer has itself a large buffer memory, the effect may be negligible. /U:1 and /M:2 are default values that are best left alone unless you want to experiment. The numbers that can be used can range from 1 to 255, and they control the timing of switching over from computing to printing and from printing to computing.

At the end of a PRINT document, the printer takes a new page so as to separate the documents that are being printed. In addition, PRINT allows the use of a queue of files.

Example
PRINT TXT1 TXT2 TXT3 TXT4

– would cause all four of these files to be printed, with a blank sheet of paper separating each pair of documents. You can add more files to the queue while PRINT is operating by using /P.

Example
PRINT TXT5/P

– adds the file TXT5 to the existing queue if there is space for it. With the default value of 10 files in the queue, this is seldom a problem. Strictly speaking, the use of /P is necessary only if /C has previously been used.

You can remove files from the queue by using /C or /T. The use of /C removes a file, so that if you type:

PRINT TXT4/C

– before this file has been printed, it will be removed from the queue. Using PRINT /T removes *all* files from the queue. You can use wildcards in the filename if you want to place a number of files in the queue with a short command. You can also use paths in the filenames. Be careful about queue lengths, because this and the other settings that are made when PRINT is first used, cannot be changed until the machine is reset and restarted with MS-DOS.

RECOVER

is used to obtain text files from disks which are corrupted because of bad sectors being used for storing the file, or because of problems with the file directory. Such files are likely to give Data Error Reading messages when used. The RECOVER command can be applied to a single filename or to the whole disk in a floppy drive. When a filename is specified, only the uncorrupted part of the file is recovered, and MS-DOS re-saves what is left. You will be notified as to how much has been recovered. The command cannot be used on a network.

As with all commands that operate on disks to recover files, you should have made an exact copy of the disk, damage included, by using DISKCOPY (see earlier, this chapter). A wildcardcan be used as a filename, but only the first matching file will be recovered.

Example
RECOVER B:MYOLD.TXTwill give a typical message of:

Press any key to begin recovery of the file(s) on drive B:
1760 of 2230 bytes recovered

When RECOVER is applied to a complete disk, all of the files on that disk are recovered, whether they are corrupted or not, and are renamed as FILE0001.REC, FILE0002.REC and so on. The message at the end of the command tells you how many files have been recovered.

Example
RECOVER B: will give typical messages of:

Press any key to begin recovery of the file(s) on drive B:
15 file(s) recovered

If your floppy disk contains directories, the saved files will be put into the root directory. Each directory on the disk will be treated as a file (which it is), and if there is no space on the root directory for more files you will get a message to that effect so that you can then copy the recovered files to another disk, delete them from the corrupted disk and use RECOVER again.

REPLACE

is a command (V3.2 onwards) that allows for another method of making selective backups by replacing or adding files from one drive/directory to another. The command requires you to specify one path and filename, followed by a path that ends with a directory. The filename that is specified in the source drive or directory will then be used to replace a file of the same name in the second drive or directory, the destination. If no such file exists in the destination directory, the command stops with a message to this effect (No files replaced). A wildcardfile specification can be used for the source file, so that several files can be replaced in a backup action.

The options of the command allow for the addition of the specified file to the destination directory, replacement over a range of sub-directories, for prompts (Y/N for each replacement), for replacement of files that have the Read-only attribute set (see ATTRIB, this chapter), and for waiting for a disk to be inserted so that single drive users are catered for.

Example
REPLACE C:\WORDS\CHAP1.TXT BOOK

- will look for the file CHAP1.TXT in the BOOK directory, and replace this with the file copy in the WORDS directory.

Example
REPLACE C:\TEXT*.TXT A:

- will replace any files with the TXT extension on the A drive with the TXT files from the TEXT directory. The options letters are /A, /P, /R, /S, and /W. All are placed after the destination drive or directory name.

The option allows the file from the source drive or directory to be added to the destination if no such file exists to be replaced. If a matching file exists, then *nothing* is done.

Example
REPLACE A:MYDATA.DAT B:/A

- will add the file MYDATA.DAT to the disk in the B drive unless the file is already present on that disk.

The /P option will cause a prompt:

Replace (mydata.dat) (Y/N)?

to be issued for each file.

The /R option will allow files to be replaced even if they are marked as read-only files by using the ATTRIB command.

The /S option will make the destination directory include all subdirectories, and if a drive is specified, all directories on the drive.

Example
REPLACE A:/CHAP?.TXT B:\ /S

will use the specified files (with a wildcard) to replace any files of matching name stored at any part of the disk in the B drive.

The /W option allows the process to be interrupted and a message issued so that you can change from the source disk to the destination disk on a single-floppy system.

REPLACE returns ERRORLEVEL codes that can be used in a batch file, see Chapter 4.

RESTORE

replaces files to the hard disk that were backed up to floppy disks by using BACKUP. Version 3.3 allows this to be from another hard disk if the files were backed up on to the hard disk by BACKUP. You can opt to restore a single file, a directory, or the entire contents of the floppies.

RESTORE must not be used when the commands APPEND, ASSIGN, JOIN or SUBST have been in use.

The options of RESTORE are:
/A:dd-mm-yy restore files carrying this or later date (V.3.3 on).
/B:dd-mm-yy restore files carrying this or earlier date (V.3.3 on).
/N restore files that were deleted (V.3.3 on).
/M restore files that have been altered or deleted (V.3.3 on).
/P do not restore a file that has been changed since backing-up. This avoids replacing a new version of a file with an old one, and should *always* be used unless the new file is known to be corrupted.
/S restore a complete directory structure, including files and subdirectories.

MS-DOS versions from 3.3 also allows the L and E options which are followed by the time, allowing you to restore files made on or later than the specified time or on or earlier than the specified time, using the same syntax as /A and /B.

Example
RESTORE C:\WP\TEXT\chap1.doc

– asks for first floppy disk to be inserted, then press any key. The screen will show the date of the backup, then a message about successful backup. You will be prompted to change floppy disks if this is needed (remember that the disks should have been numbered in order of use when BACKUP was used).

Example
RESTORE C:WP/P

– restores files that belong to this directory and have not been changed since backing up.

SELECT

is used to make a system disk (floppy) that carries information specific to a country. This allows for different versions of a word-processor, for example, to be made for corresponding with different countries. When such a disk is used for starting the computer, the correct information for the selected country will be loaded, so that the currency, time and date conventions are correct, and the keyboard will also be correctly configured. Versions of MS-DOS prior to 3.3 use SELECT differently, and it is not implemented before 3.0.

The V.3.3 SELECT uses drive letter, followed by a drive or path for the system files and then the country and keyboard codes in that order.

Example
SELECT A: B: 044 UK

– will take system tracks and data from drive A and place the system tracks on drive B, using the UK country code (044) and UK keyboard. The disk will be formatted, and the files will be copied, including a CONFIG.SYS file (see Chapter 6) with the COUNTRY = 044 line, and an AUTOEXEC.BAT file with KEYB UK 850.

When SELECT is used on V.3.0 to 3.2, the command is followed by the country code and keyboard letters only. The source of files must be a system disk placed in drive A:, and the destination will be a disk in Drive B:.

Example
```
SELECT 044 UK
```

– will place the system tracks on to the disk in drive B, and also a CONFIG.SYS file that contains COUNTRY = 044 and an AUTOEXEC.BAT file that contains KEYBUK as one of its lines.

SHARE

is used for networked systems so that files can be shared by each computer on the network. For each file, MS-DOS will allocate a sharing code which is used to decide which users can make use of the file. SHARE allows memory to be set aside for the sharing codes. When a program that is running on one machine in a network is using a file, it may use SHARE to put a lock on that file so that no other user has access in that time. The other function of SHARE is to allocate memory for locking codes.

Example
```
SHARE
```

– prepare for file sharing using default values of 2K for sharing codes and enough memory for 20 locks.

Example
```
SHARE/F:256/S:30
```

– provides for 256 paragraphs of 16 bytes = 4K of memory for sharing, and 30 locks.

SORT

is used mainly as a filter, requiring input and output to be specified. See Chapter 6 for details which apply also to SORT used other than for filtering.

SUBST

allows you to substitute a letter for a valid but unused drive in the place of a path. The letter that is used must be valid, and this may require the use of LASTDRIVE (see Chapter 3) to allow the use of letters beyond the default of E: to be used for drive letters.

SUBST should be used only if you *must* keep an old program in service, with no up-date available, because SUBST cannot be used along with ASSIGN, BACKUP, DISKCOMP, DISKCOPY, FDISK, FORMAT, JOIN, LABEL or RESTORE. The preferred method is to use programs designed to work with directories, and avoid the use of SUBST altogether.

Example
```
SUBST E: \WORDS\BOOK
```

– makes the path \WORDS\BOOK behave as if it were a separate drive with letter E:, allowing you to save to or load from this drive E: as if it were a disk drive in its own right. This allows you to have your word processor program chapters in a subdirectory such as \WORDS and its text files in another subdirectory of WORDS called BOOK; but using filenames such as E:Chap1.txt when you save text. Such text will then be stored and will appear in the directory as if you had used:

```
\WORDS\BOOK\Chap1.txt
```

directly with a program that accepted path names in the filenames.

To remove substitution, use the /D option.

Example
```
SUBST E: /D
```

– removes the substitution on the E: drive letter.

SYS

transfers the hidden DOS and IO files to a formatted disk provided that room has been made for them during formatting. This is done either by using SYS on a formatted but unwritten disk, or one that has been formatted with /S or /B options to make space for the system files. SYS cannot be used on a disk that has been formatted in the ordinary way and then has files recorded on to it.

Example
```
SYS B:
```

– transfers system files to disk in drive B, which should have been formatted using /B or /S.

TREE

Displays the list of directories from root to branch.

The list can be very lengthy and should be printed. No files are shown unless the /F option is used.

There are several utilities that produce better print-outs than TREE. Among them is the public-domain utility TREED, which produces a pictorial diagram of the directory structure.

Example
```
TREE C:
```

– shows the directory tree starting from the root directory of C: but not showing the files in each directory. The printout is of the form:

```
Path: C:/WSTAR
Sub-directories: BOOKS
                 LETTERS
                 PROPOSAL
                 OLDTXT
Path: C:\WSTAR\BOOKS
Sub-directories: DOSBOOK
                 WINDOWS
```

– and each path is treated in this way.

XCOPY

is an enhanced file copier which allows for selective copying of files that have archive bits set, or according to date. The main advantage of XCOPY, however, is that it can create a copy which has the same directory structure as the original disk. Unlike BACKUP, XCOPY produces files that can be used in the normal way, with no compression, but this means, of course, that a much larger number of floppies would be needed to achieve backup of a hard disk as compared to the use of BACKUP. In addition, because XCOPY tests the archive attribute of a file (see ATTRIB), it can be used in a batch file to ensure that files that have just been created are correctly backed up without backing up files that have *not* been altered.

The XCOPY command is followed by the source and the destination drives and paths (if applicable), along with up to 8 option letters if these are needed. Wildcards are permitted for the source files.

Example
```
XCOPY C:\WORDS\*.* A:
```

– will copy all the files from the WORDS directory

and any of its sub-directories on to the disk in the A: drive, preserving the sub-directory structure of the original.

The option letters are /A, /D, /E, /M, /P, /S, /V, and /W, all of which are used following the destination drive and path.

The /A option ensures that only files that have their archive bit set (see ATTRIB, this chapter) will be copied. Using /A does *not* reset the archive bit, so that when archive bit copying is used it is nearly always in conjunction with /M.

The /D option is followed by a colon and a date, so that only files which have been created or changed on or following this date will be copied.

The /E option must accompany the /S option, and it allows empty sub-directories to be copied as well as those which contain files.

The /M option copies only files which have the archive bit set, and will reset the archive bit after copying so that the same file will not be copied again unless it has been altered.

The /P option causes the system to ask for confirmation of each copy in the form:

```
C:\WORDS\CHAP1.TXT (Y/N)?
```

so that you can check each copy and determine for yourself whether or not to proceed.

The /S option allows files to be copied from a directory and also from all of the sub-directories of that directory. This can be very useful when a wildcardis being used in the file name.

The /V option will verify each copy after it is written to check that it is identical to the original.

The /W option will prompt you to swap disks during copying, so that XCOPY can be used with a single-floppy machine.

Example

```
XCOPY C:\BOOKS\*.TXT A:/M/S
```

– will make copies of all files with the *TXT* extension from directory BOOKs and any of its sub-directories, copying only the files whose archive bits are set, and resetting the bits after copying so that no further backup will take place unless the files are subsequently changed.

6 Pipes, filters, redirection and configuration

Redirection

Redirection means the transfer of data from one output or input device to an alternative. The data will normally be the output from a program which would normally be directed to the screen, or the input to a program which would normally be taken from the keyboard (assuming that all such inputs can be put into a file – this could mean finding a file editor that could work with Ctrl – characters)

Redirection in MS-DOS makes use of the signs ⟩ and ⟨ to indicate the direction of the flow of data, with ⟩ meaning a redirection of *output* and ⟨ meaning a redirection of *input*. Looking at output redirection first, the form of the command is:

```
command ) output device
```

– which makes use of the usual abbreviations for the output devices. The most common requirement is redirection of screen output to a file or redirection to a printer. For a file redirection, the filename will have to be specified, for a parallel printer, use PRN. There *must* be a space on the pointed side of the ⟩ sign.

Example
```
DIR C:\wp\text) dirfil.doc
```

– will put the directory of C:\wp\text into a file called dirfil.doc. This file can then be used like any ASCII file, so that it can be read into a word processor etc.

Example
```
TYPE B:blurb.txt) prn
```

– will print the file blurb.txt on the parallel printer (the printer must be wired up and switched on).

Example
```
TYPE A:other.doc) aux
```

– will send the file *other.doc* to the serial port, to a serial printer or another computer. The serial port must have been correctly set up using MODE. The use of AUX and COM1 is interchangeable (you might have to specify COM2 if this is the serial port you use). This redirection works satisfactorily both with serial printers and with direct-links to other computers, rather like using COPY *filename* AUX.

Using the redirection sign 〉〉 has the effect of appending data to an existing text file.

Example
```
DIR B:〉〉 prnfil.doc
```

– will add the directory of the disk in the B: drive to the file prnfil.doc (in the current drive) without deleting the present contents of the file.

Another 'device' that can be used for redirection is NUL. When this is used, the output of the program 'disappears', it is not displayed on screen nor printed. This can be used as a way of testing that something will be read correctly, and also as a way of making sure that an output from an action that is carried out in a batch file does not cause any screen output (as it would even with ECHO OFF used).

Example
```
DIR A:〉 NUL
```

– will read the directory of the disk in drive A and consign it to oblivion. The disk drive motor is the only indication that something has happened.

The input redirection is less often used in such straightforward ways, because it is seldom necessary to redirect an input. If an input is needed from the serial port it is always better to use a communications program, because the use of AUX or COM as sources of *input* is not necessarily supported, and there is the problem of transferring the end-of-file character. One possible exception to the use of redirection in inputs is taking inputs from a file. If a program requires a number of commands that are delivered from the keyboard as you start it up, these can *possibly* be taken instead from a file in which each command has been put on a separate line. The problem is to find a program that will accept such redirection, and many popular programs do not, or if they do, can hang up at the end of the file. It is often necessary to use an editor that can place Ctrl and Esc characters into the file, and in this respect the word-processor PC-Write (obtainable at one time as shareware) is very useful. In general, it is better to avoid input redirection except into Filter programs, see later. The MS-DOS commands that accept keyboard inputs will all accept redirection. This redirection ceases when the file ends.

Example
```
TIME <CONFIL.DOC
```

– will alter the time setting, reading a time that has been stored in the file CONFIL.DOC on the current drive.

Redirections generally should be confined to directing outputs to the parallel printer or to a file, and for redirecting an input to a filter, because other actions do not necessarily work well or reliably.

Pipes and filters

A pipe is a method of transferring data from one program to another, and is the preferred way of getting the output of a file to affect the input of another. The syntax is to use the ¦ sign between the programs which are to be connected in this way. Once again, however, the programs that accept input data from a pipe are usually the MS-DOS commands or other programs written for the purpose. These latter programs are the *filters*, and their purpose is to alter the output from or the input to a program.

Piping is achieved by creating a temporary disk file, so that you cannot operate piping if your disks are all write-protected or if they are full. The file that is created is called %PIPEX.$$$, which is, intentionally, not the sort of snazzy title that you would want for your own files. This ensures that there is little or no chance that the file of that name will already exist on the disk when a pipe is created, because the pipe file is deleted immediately following the pipe action, leaving no trace on the disk.

The filter programs that are usually supplied with DOS are FIND, MORE and SORT, of which FIND can be used for purposes that are separate from piping. All three are external commands, meaning that they are programs which have to be on a disk in the current drive or on a path which can be searched. The effect of the filter is to select or rearrange data which has been piped to it by a program, and then pass that modified data on to another program by way of a pipe, or to a printer by way of a redirection. Most filter programs are used in conjunction with TYPE or DIR, the two MS-DOS commands which provide an output of text.

FIND

FIND is a good example to take in order to demonstrate the difference between program use and filter use.

```
1 FIND "Spotless" textfill.txt
2 TYPE textfill.txtFIND "Spotless"
```

The first example uses FIND as a program whose output will appear on the screen. The second example uses TYPE to pass text to FIND used as a filter, with the result again appearing on the screen. Used as a program, FIND is followed by the phrase to be found and also the filename.

Used as a filter, FIND appears following the pipe sign ¦, and is itself followed only by the phrase that is to be found. The text that is to be searched by the FIND filter has to be passed along the pipe from another program, and in this case TYPE has been used as a way of selecting the text. Normally, TYPE would display the text on the screen, but with FIND interposed between the TYPE command and the screen output, only the selected output is shown.

Remember that FIND, like the other filter programs, is external, so that the program must be present on the current drive or on a directory which will be searched, using a PATH line in the AUTOEXEC.BAT file.

The use of FIND as a filter makes it of considerably wider use than FIND used only as a program. For example, suppose that the root directory of your hard disk contains several hundred files (which is bad organisation, but that's another matter). To find files created in 1987 we can use:

```
DIR C:¦FIND "87"
```

because each date is stored in the form DD-MM-YY (unless you have forgotten to use the COUNTRY file to adapt to UK date conventions).

FIND allows three option letters /C, /N, and /V which are placed between FIND and the item to be found.

The /C option alters the output of FIND to a count of the number of lines in which the item is found.

The /N option prints out a line number as well as the line that contains the item.

The /V option displays the lines that do *not* contain the search item.

MORE

The MORE filter simply cuts text into pages which can be displayed on the screen. If data is sent to the screen through the MORE filter, then one screen full of data will be displayed at a time, with the message

`--More--`

appearing at the bottom of the screen. The next page can then be displayed by pressing any key. To send a text file through this filter, you have to specify that the contents of the file will be piped to the filter, and if the command that is used to provide the text would normally send it to the screen, then so also is the output of MORE sent to the screen.

Example
`TYPE READ.ME : MORE`

– will place the contents of the file READ.ME on the screen, one page at a time, assuming that the MORE program is on the same disk as READ.ME.
   You could, of course, then redirect the output to the printer by using the command in the form:

`TYPE READ.ME : MORE > PRN`

and an alternative is:

`MORE < READ.ME > PRN`

which uses redirection rather than piping. Note the different order, also that the TYPE command is not needed because the < sign implies that the file READ.ME is used as an input to MORE.

SORT

SORT is the other standard filter, and its effect is to arrange text data in alphabetical order of the letter in the first column (and when two words have the same first letter, then the second letter will be taken into account and so on).

Example
`DIR:SORT`

– will place on to the screen a directory of the current disk or directory which is sorted in alphabetical order. The output of DIR has in this example been piped through SORT, and then to the screen.

Example
```
TYPE INXIT¦SORT
```

– when INXIT consists of a list of names in any order, will produce a sorted list on the screen.

The SORT command and filter allow options which can be a number or the letter R, placed immediately following SORT and separated by the usual stroke mark.

The /5 option will sort the file by the order of the character in the 5th column, in this example. Any valid column number can be used. This can be useful if the list consists of four places for numbers, a comma, and then a word.

The /R option sorts the items in reverse order, highest value first and then to lowest.

Combined pipe, filter and redirection

The actions of piping, filtering and redirection can be combined, as long as the correct order of writing filenames and symbols is observed. A few examples have already been illustrated.

Example
```
DIR¦SORT > ALPHADIR.TXT
```

– will sort a directory into order and then send the results to a file called ALPHADIR.TXT so that when you TYPE or PRINT the file ALPHADIR.TXT, you will find that the directory is in alphabetical order. You could equally easily have directed the alphabetical listing to the printer by using PRN in place of the filename in the example above.

Another common requirement is to take data from one file, sort it, and then file under another filename. This has already been illustrated, but it can bear mentioning again.

Example
```
SORT < OLDFIL > NEWFIL
```

– will take the output from the file OLDFIL, filter it through SORT and then send the sorted result to the file called NEWFIL. SORT is in this example being used as a program along with redirection.

Use in batch-file utilities

The use of piping, filters and redirection is

particularly valuable in batch files, because once you have constructed the batch file with all of its commands, you can use it for any files that you need to exercise these actions on. One example is an indexing program. This is intended for indexing words in a book, so that each entry consists of a word or phrase, then a comma, and then a page number.

The file provides for calling up a simple editor (the RPED editor which comes with the Amstrad machines) to create the list of words and page numbers, and then recording this. The file is then sorted into order, and recorded again so that it can finally be processed by a word-processor. The form of the batch file allows you to use it in the form:

```
INDX TXTFIL.TXT
```

for a new index, or in the form:

```
INDX OLDTXT.FIL NEWTXT.FIL
```

when an old index has to be extended.

```
echo off
cd\textutil
echo Is this a new index?
yn
if errorlevel 1 goto oldie
del tmpind
rped tmpind
sort < tmpind > %1
goto endit
:oldie
rped %1 tmpind
sort < tmpind > %2
:endit
cd\wstar
ws
cd\
```

This asks if the index is new so that if a very long index had been recorded half-way through, it could be resumed. If the index is a new one the temporary file *tmpind* is deleted (it might not exist on the disk, but this does not matter), and the RPED editor program is then called to create a file called *tmpind*. Once this has been created, and after leaving RPED, the SORT line arranges the index into alphabetical order and files this under the filename that was supplied for use with a new index. The GOTO

ENDIT line then moves to the set of lines which call up the word processor (WordStar in this case) so that the index can be put easily into printable form.

For an old index, both old and new names have been provided, and jumping to label *:oldie* will cause RPED to be called with instructions to read the first file and, when finished, to save under the filename *tmpind*. The usual sort then follows, and the file is recorded under the second name that was supplied in the command line for the batch file. The word processor is then called up as before.

Another use of piping is to overcome the inability of some commands to accept wildcards. One well-known example is FIND, so that FIND is not particularly useful for directory lists, but if a listing of a complete directory is obtained from CHKDSK (so that all files can be read), then FIND can be used as a filter to locate specific parts of a filename, such as the extension (but without using the wildcard-characters). As an example:

```
CHKDSK/B ¦ FIND ".TXT" ¦ SORT ¦ MORE
```

will obtain all the file and sub-directory names, pass them to FIND so that the extension TXT can be located, and then SORT to put into order. Since this is likely to be used on a hard disk, MORE is added to page the output.

The extension name could be passed to this in a batch file by using %1 in the usual way, but whatever is typed in the command line *must* be in capitals.

The CONFIG.SYS file

The CONFIG.SYS file is, like the AUTOEXEC.BAT file, a file of lines of commands in ASCII text, and is used when the computer is started up, before the AUTOEXEC.BAT file is run. The CONFIG.SYS file is more specialised than the AUTOEXEC.BAT file, however, and it cannot be run on its own after the computer has been started up, unlike the AUTOEXEC.BAT file.

A few commands can be used either in the CONFIG.SYS file or the AUTOEXEC.BAT file, but most of the CONFIG.SYS commands can be used only within the CONFIG.SYS file. The most important feature of the CONFIG.SYS file is that it allows you to set up several important features of MS-DOS use, such as files and buffers, along with installing device drivers, files which allow specific devices to be used.

My own CONFIG.SYS file for an Amstrad PC 1512 (with 32M hard disk card) is as shown here:

```
files=20
lastdrive=H
buffers=5
device=ramdrive.sys nvr
country=044
```

and it's likely that you would want to use at least this number of lines, probably more, and probably with different entries if you do not use the Amstrad machine. The most complicated command form of CONFIG.SYS is DEVICE, so that the DEVICE command will be considered last in this list.

BREAK

is used along with ON or OFF in the form:

```
BREAK = ON
```

in the CONFIG.SYS file. The BREAK command can also be used as an internal command, and can be included in the AUTOEXEC.BAT file. The effect of BREAK = ON is to extend checks of the keyboard for the use of the Ctrl-Break keys, allowing disk operations to be broken off, but slowing the action of the computer. The BREAK command is internal, so that no system disk or MS-DOS files need be present to implement BREAK.

BUFFERS

By using a line such as BUFFERS=5, the number of 512-bit memory buffers that MS-DOS can use is made equal to 5. The default on versions of MS-DOS prior to 3.3 was only 2 buffers, but on V.3.3, the number of default buffers is made proportional to the amount of RAM installed. Some disk-cacheing programs (such as SpeedRead, supplied with the Western Digital filecards) create additional buffers, and allow you to use a small number of buffers in the CONFIG.SYS file. If you do not use any cache type of program, it can be an advantage to use a large number of buffers. Up to 99 buffers can be specified in a BUFFERS=nn type of line. Each buffer requires 528 bytes of memory to set up, and for programs that do not use a lot of random-access filing, two buffers is often adequate. Program manuals will usually indicate if they require a special BUFFERS setting, so that you should set your CONFIG.SYS file to a BUFFERS number that will suit the most demanding program. BUFFERS is an internal command.

COUNTRY

has a different configuration according to whether you use a DOS version before 3.3 or not. In DOS 3.0 to 3.2, the COUNTRY command line used no options, and the UK version was:

```
COUNTRY = 044
```

in which the code number 044 is simply the international telephone dialling number for dialling **into** the UK. By specifying this number, the date, time and currency conventions for the UK can be used in MS-DOS and in programs that make use of MS-DOS.

On V3.3 and later, COUNTRY can take two additional options. These include a code page (there are two code pages for each country) and a country information file. If nothing is specified, the defaults are Code Page 437 and file COUNTRY.SYS. The use of Code Pages is restricted to two printers (IBM 4201 and 5202) and display systems (EGA and LCD) that support the system.

Note that COUNTRY is an external program, so that if it appears in the CONFIG.SYS file, there has to be a copy of COUNTRY.SYS in the current directory. You **cannot** make use of a PATH command in the AUTOEXEC.BAT file, because CONFIG.SYS is run before AUTOEXEC.BAT is read.

Example
```
COUNTRY = 044,850,C:\MSDOS\COUNTRY.SYS
```

– establishes the country code number as 044 (the UK), and the code page (for suitable printers and screens) as 850. The file path to COUNTRY.SYS is given, since no PATH command can be used.

DISPLAY.SYS

is provided with DOS 3.3 on to allow code page switching on EGA and LCD screen types. See under DEVICE for details of use.

DRIVER

The DRIVER.SYS file is used along with DEVICE, see below. Its purpose is to allow any type of disk drive that is supported by MS-DOS to be used with your computer. More details of DRIVER.SYS are included under DEVICE.

DRIVEPARM

is not a standard MS-DOS command, but it has appeared with several versions of DOS, particularly for Amstrad machines. DRIVEPARM allows one drive to be configured so that it differs from the normal specification (for the other drive in a twin-drive machine, for example). The form of the command is:

DRIVEPARM = /D:2/F:2/T:80

– and this example is typical if you are converting a twin 5.25" machine to use one 3.5" drive in place of the B: drive. The option letters are shown below, with n used to mean a single digit:

/T:nnn	Tracks per side, 1 to 999
/S:nn	Sectors per side, 1 to 99
/H:nn	Maximum head number, 1 to 99
/C	Doorlock support needed
/N	non-removable block device
/F:n	Form factor, 0 to 7, using:
	0 = 5.25"
	1 = 5.25" 1.2 M capacity
	2 = 720K
	3 = 8" single density
	4 = 8" double density
	5 = Hard disk
	6 = Tape drive
	7 = Other

FCBS

is important if you run a networked system in which files are shared or if you are using programs that were written for an old version of MS-DOS. The form of the command, which can be used only in the CONFIG.SYS file, is:

FCBS = 12,6

meaning that up to 12 files can be manipulated at once, and 6 must be left open, so that these files cannot be closed by anyone else on the network.

FILES

The line FILES = 20 allows 20 files to be manipulated at any one time. For each file that has been opened, MS-DOS allocates a 16-bit number, called the file handle. The default is 8, but some programs, particularly word-processors, require more files to be worked, and if no additional file handles are available, the message:

`No free file handles`

will be delivered, causing restrictions on what can be done. By using a line such as FILES = 20, the number of file handles can be increased, with very little expense in the amount of memory used, only 39 bytes for each file handle above the statutory 8.

LASTDRIVE

is used to declare the letter that will be used for the last *logical* drive. This is normally E, but if you want to use the SUBST command (despite all of the warnings) then you can allocate more letters for drives, up to Z, with a command such as:

`LASTDRIVE = K`

LASTDRIVE can also be very useful if you want to partition a hard disk in several sections (see FDISK, Chapter 5), or make use of expanded memory to set up a RAMdisk or more than one RAMdisk.

PRINTER.SYS

is supplied with DOS 3.3 onwards to provide for the use of the printers (IBM printers) which support the use of Code Pages. See DEVICE, below, for details of the use of `PRINTER.SYS`

RAMDRIVE

is used to set up a RAMdisk, and is found on the MS-DOS distribution disk of Amstrad machines. For its use, see DEVICE below.

SHELL

is very unlikely to be used unless you have very specialised interests. It allows the COMMAND.COM program to be by-passed in favour of another form of command processor, and the form of the command is:

```
SHELL = MYCOM.COM
```

assuming that a program called MYCOM.COM is available for use in this way.

VDISK.SYS

is the standard MS-DOS method of creating a RAMdisk, using a portion of the RAM as if it were a disk drive. For details, see DEVICE, below.

DEVICE

is the command which calls up 'device drivers'. In early versions of MS-DOS, routines had to be incorporated into the operating system to allow the use of various graphics boards and printers, and because the number of such routines soon became excessive, the principle was adopted of leaving the core of the commands unchanged and adapting for different devices (CGA, EGA, VGA, and all the varieties of printers) by using separate programs, called device drivers. This also allowed for other types of device, such as RAMdisk to be provided for. DEVICE can be used only within a CONFIG.SYS file, but there can be several DEVICE command lines in a single CONFIG.SYS file, each used to configure a different type of device.

The form of a DEVICE command is:

```
DEVICE = filename
```

in which a full filename with path and extension can be used if needed. In general, the filenames that will be used have the extension SYS, and not all of the possible program files will be included on your MS-DOS distribution disk. You can buy additional SYS files for use in the DEVICE command, and there are several public domain device files available. We shall look at some of the more common MS-DOS SYS files, starting with the screen handler, ANSI.SYS.

ANSI.SYS

Using the line:

```
DEVICE = ANSI.SYS
```

in the CONFIG.SYS file loads in the ANSI screen handler. This does *not* mean any change to any of the programs that make use of DOS, because software such as word-processors, spreadsheets and databases use their own screen-control routines, but for use of DOS itself and for some programs, such as some versions of BASIC, the facilities of ANSI.SYS can be very convenient. Though ANSI.SYS is described as a screen handler, it also allows a considerable amount of manipulation of the keyboard, so that while using DOS you can assign keys (particularly the function keys) to various uses.

When the ANSI.SYS line has been used in the CONFIG.SYS file, the pattern of screen and keyboard can be changed by typing commands, all of which start with the ESC key. This means, for most users, that these commands cannot be entered directly, because MS-DOS uses the ESC key to terminate a command and move to the next line. Direct commands to ANSI therefore have to be made by way of the PROMPT command (see Chapter 3), which can make use of $e to mean the ESC code.

Example
```
PROMPT $e[2J
```

– clears the screen, and leaves *no prompt* remaining. If you need to have the prompt restored, the necessary characters must be added in another prompt line.

Example
```
PROMPT $e[2J
PROMPT $p $t
```

– clears the screen and gives a prompt that consists of directory and time. Note that if you use PROMPT $e[2J $p $t you will clear the screen and get a prompt, but each time you press RETURN the screen will be cleared, since the use of PROMPT makes screen-clearing part of the prompt that appears each time RETURN is pressed.

If ANSI commands have to be set up as a matter of routine, they can be read from a file. Such a file must, however, be written by an editor which will put the ESC character into place, and not all editors will do this because many interpret the ESC key to mean 'end of editing'. A few editors will allow codes, rather like the $e code of PROMPT, to place an ESC character (ASCII 27) into a file. You can, however, write a batch file in which the ANSI commands are placed in prompt form, using $e to mean the ESC character. The EDLIN editor which is supplied with MS-DOS will place ESC characters into a file, but this Editor is primitive, and needs considerable experience.

Users of WordStar, certainly of WordStar 4.0, can place the ESC character into files in a fairly simple way:

1 Start a non-document file, using whatever filename you want.
2 Write the file, using a substitute character for ESC. The substitute can be any character that is not used in ANSI commands, such as @.
3 Use the search and replace command. Type the substitute character when asked what to search for, and when asked what to replace with, type Ctrl-P Esc (Ctrl and P, then Esc keys). This will place the ^[symbols on the screen, and the bracket is in addition to the bracket that appears in each ANSI code, so that the clear screen command will look like: ^[[2J.
4 Save the file as usual. Note that though the Esc character shows on screen as ^[, you cannot obtain this character by typing ^[from the keyboard.

The ANSI command codes are listed below, with the ESC character omitted since there is no standard method of showing it. You will need to remember, then, that each sequence shown will start with $e if you are using a PROMPT line to put in the code. In the following list, j and k are used to mean numbers of up to 2 digits. Note that the case of letters is important, so that you cannot substitute j for J, for example.

[jA	move cursor up j rows, unless already at top.
[jB	move cursor down j rows, unless already at bottom.
[jC	move cursor right j columns, unless at RHS.

`[jD`	move cursor left j columns, unless already at LHS.
`[j;kf`	move cursor to row j column k.
`[j;kH`	move cursor to row j column k.
`[=jh`	set screen width and parameters.
`[2J`	clear screen, cursor to top left corner.
`[K`	erase to end of line
`[=jl`	reset screen width and parameters (note: letter ell)
`[j;m`	set graphics.
`[6n`	print cursor position.
`[j;kp`	redefine key
`[j;kR`	cursor to row j column k and print this position.
`[s`	save cursor position.
`[u`	restore cursor position.

Screen width and parameters for ESC[=jh command

Value of j	Effect
0	40 column × 25 rows monochrome
1	40 × 25 colour
2	80 × 25 monochrome
3	80 × 25 colour
4	320 dots per line × 200 lines per screen colour
5	320 × 200 monochrome
6	640 × 200 monochrome
7	wrap at end of each line

Graphics parameters numbers

Number	Effect
0	all graphics controls off
1	bold on
2	faint on
3	italic on
4	underscore on (not on colour type of display)
5	slow blink on
6	rapid blink on
7	inverse video on (foreground/background colours reversed)
8	concealed on (not displayed – useful for passwords)
30	black foreground
31	red foreground
32	green foreground

33	yellow foreground
34	blue foreground
35	magenta foreground
36	cyan foreground
37	white foreground
40	black background
41	red background
42	green background
44	yellow background
44	blue background
45	magenta background
46	cyan background
47	white background
48	subscript
49	superscript

Note: some implementations of ANSI may not accept all of the codes shown in this table.

Example The file shown below is a batch file that will clear the screen, and write a headline in bold flashing text, then return to normal.

```
prompt $e[2J
prompt $e[1;5m
prompt
ECHO THIS IS THE HEADLINE
prompt $e[0m
prompt
```

The snag here is that it uses ECHO for placing text on the screen, and you cannot use ECHO OFF at the start of the file, otherwise the prompt commands have no effect. It is much better, if you need to place text on a screen, to use a word-processor such as WordStar which can put in the ESC sequences, as described earlier, and use batch files only for making changes which are then used to affect TYPE commands, for example. However, another way round the problem is simply to use a PROMPT line to display the text, as long as this is cancelled when you need to have a prompt symbol used.

Keyboard reassignment is made using the ESC[..p command, and this requires both keycodes and a set of characters to be supplied. The keycode must be a number or pair of numbers, and the characters can be placed in the command as ASCII codes or in string form, such as "WORDSTAR". The function keys are referred to by using a two-number code with a zero as the first number, and numbers 59-68 as the second number.

Example
`Esc[109;77;83;45;68;79;83p`

– will redefine the *m* key(ASCII 109) to produce
`MS-DOS`. You then have to avoid typing *prompt* and
use PROMPT (or proMpt) instead!

Example
`Esc[0;59;"This is F1";13p`

– will redefine F1 to give `This is F1` followed by a
carriage return.

Example
`Esc[0,84;"This is SHIFT F1";13p`

– will redefine SHIFT F1 to give the phrase `This is
SHIFT F1`.

Function key codes – these are the number
following 0; in the ANSI codes.

Key	Alone	Shift	Ctrl	Alt
F1	59	84	94	104
F2	60	85	95	105
F3	61	86	96	106
F4	62	87	97	107
F5	63	88	98	108
F6	64	89	99	109
F7	65	90	100	110
F8	66	91	101	111
F9	67	92	102	112
F10	68	93	103	113

Note that there are some later versions of ANSI.SYS
in the public domain, such as NANSI.SYS.

DISPLAY.SYS

The use of DISPLAY.SYS started in DOS 3.3 in
order to implement code page switching on screen
types that support this feature. These screen types are
EGA (including PS/2 Video Display Adapter) and
LCD (for portable machines). Other types of video
display cannot make use of DISPLAY.SYS. Earlier
versions of MS-DOS used files called code pages in
order to hold data on displayed characters for
different languages. The US code page was numbered
437, and versions of MS-DOS for export would use
860, 863 or 865.

Later, a multi-language code page 850 was

introduced and used in DOS 3.3 onwards. Code page switching was introduced with DOS 3.3 in order to be able to accommodate software that was written using the earlier code pages other than 850. Some code pages are built into the device driver files, and are referred to as hardware code pages. Others can be obtained from software files (the .CPI files) and selected by way of a MODE command such as:

```
MODE CON CODEPAGE PREPARE = ((860,850)C:\
ega.cpi)
```

and these are known as *prepared* code pages (see MODE, Chapter 5)

The DISPLAY.SYS line is typically:

```
DEVICE = DISPLAY.SYS CON = (ega,850,2,2)
```

– to use the EGA video board with code page 850, two prepared code pages, and two fonts. The fonts number can be omitted, and is not needed for the LCD video adapter.

DRIVER.SYS

This is the Device file which allows disk drives to be set up, and is particularly useful if you alter the pattern of disk drive on a machine by adding an external drive or by replacing one kind of internal drive by another (such as replacing a 5.25" drive by a 3.5" drive).

The command allows you to select a number (the physical drive number) and a latter (the logical drive letter). The difference between these two is that the number has to correspond to an actual piece of hardware; but the letter can be assigned to a RAMdrive, or as another letter affecting an existing drive. During the startup procedure, before the CONFIG.SYS file is read, the standard set-up of drives A, B and C is carried out. On a single floppy drive, both A and B are assigned to Drive 0, the floppy drive. This is how you can use the single drive to copy disks with the message about changing to the disk for the B: drive appearing. The C letter is reserved for the hard disk, but can be re-assigned to RAMdisk.

In a DRIVER.SYS line, you can specify:
1 /D:, the drive number, using 0 to 127 for floppy disks, 128 to 255 for hard drives.
2 /T: the number of tracks per side, 1 to 999,

default 80.

3 /S: the number of sectors per track, 1 to 99, default 9.

4 /H: the number of heads (maximum), 1 to 99, default 2.

5 /C – detection for drive door open.

6 /N – a fixed disk.

7 /F: type of device as:

/F:0 – floppy of 160K to 360K

/F:1 – floppy of 1.2 M

/F:2 – floppy of 720K

/F:7 – floppy of 1.44 M

Note: F:3 was formerly used for an 8″ single-density disk, and numbers 4 to 6 for double-density 8″, hard disk, and tape.

Example

DEVICE = DRIVER.SYS /D:2 /F:2

– installs an external floppy disk, drive 2, with 720K capacity (this would be a 3.5″ disk). The system will allocate a letter, probably E.

PRINTER.SYS

is used only by DOS 3.3 onwards, for installing code-page compatible printers. At the time of writing, these were the IBM 4201 and 5202 models, and printers fully compatible with these or providing emulations. For a note on code pages, see DISPLAY.SYS.

RAMDRIVE.SYS

– a RAMdisk device drive used in Amstrad machines in conjunction with a small section of fixed memory which is maintained by batteries when the machine is switched off. This is called the non-volatile RAM, or NVR. The RAMDRIVE.SYS line follows the syntax of the more standard VDISK.SYS, but allows the size of the disk to be specified in the CONFIG.SYS file or by a number stored in the NVR.

The disk size can optionally be followed by a number for sector size (default 128 bytes) and a number for root directory entries permitted (default is 64, range 2 to 1024). Adding /A allows either extended memory (in 80286 or 80386 machines) or an expanded memory board of the LIM specification to be used as a RAMdisk. For each RAMdisk that is set up, MS-DOS will allocate a drive letter, provided that LASTDRIVE has been set so as to allow a large enough range of letters.

Example
```
DEVICE = RAMDRIVE.SYS 64
```

– sets up a RAMdrive of 64K. The defaults of 128 byte sectors and 64 root directories entries can be used.

Example
```
DEVICE = RAMDRIVE.SYS NVR
```

– reads the RAMdrive size from the non-volatile memory of the Amstrad machine.

Example
```
DEVICE = RAMDRIVE.SYS 512 256 256 /A
```

– sets up a 512K ramdrive with 256 byte sectors and 256 directory entries using expanded LIM memory.

VDISK

is the more standard version of the RAMdisk driver. The syntax uses the same set of numbers for size, bytes per sector, and number of root directory entries as RAMDRIVE above. The option /E is used to specify extended memory of up to 4M, and there is an option to alter the number of sectors that will be transferred at a time, default 8.

Example
```
DEVICE = VDISK.SYS 1024 /E:4
```

– sets up a 1M (1024K) RAMdisk in extended memory, transferring 4 sectors at a time.

XMAEM.SYS

is present in IBM DOS 4.0 and is intended to drive expanded RAM, emulating the action of the IBM PS/2 models 70 and 80 (80286) expanded memory adapter.

XMA2EMS.SYS

is also available on DOS 4.0, and is intended to drive

the LIM type of expanded memory board as supplied by IBM.

7 MS-DOS other utilities

MS-DOS in all of its incarnations to date has included on the distribution disk several programs that are classed as programmers' utilities, rather than as internal or external commands that the majority of users would encounter. The two major utilities are EDLIN, a file text editor, and DEBUG, a memory and file investigation utility, are basic and very unfriendly programs that are intended for fast use by programmers who are experienced in their use and accustomed to their ways.

In this book, no attempt will be made to provide an extended tutorial for EDLIN, only a summary of commands and their uses. DEBUG, however, is an extremely useful program which in many cases is better for dealing with problems than some of the high-cost alternatives that are offered. DEBUG is particularly useful for dealing with the problem of a program that has 'crashed' back to DOS leaving data jammed in the memory.

EDLIN was probably never intended to be more than a hurriedly cobbled form of editor for programmers working with DOS in the early days, and it shows more than a trace of being derived from a similar editor, called ED. for CP/M. Its main trademark is the use of the prompt * which appears to show that a command is expected. The commands are cryptic and abbreviated, making them ideal for experienced programmers in a hurry, but rather less satisfactory for anyone wanting to write such items as batch files. The main strength of EDLIN is that it allows characters such as the Esc character to be put into a file, and unless your use of MS-DOS demands that you should be able to carry out such actions, then a more modern form of editor is infinitely preferable. Anyone who uses a modern version of WordStar (V.4.0 onwards) has the ability to place Esc characters into text, using the search and replace technique described in Chapter 6, so that EDLIN is not even essential for this particular task.

The DEBUG program belongs to the same era, but is one of the few programs that is readily available to explore the memory of the PC, including the ROM BIOS, though there are many programs which can work on files and disks. DEBUG allows you to carry out actions like modifying COMMAND.COM, but this should not encourage you to do so unless you are

confident that you know exactly what you are doing.
The golden rule is *never* to work on the main copy
of anything, and when a modified program is tested,
make sure that there are backup copies of the original
version available. Remember that if you have
problems with a floppy disk, then you can make an
exact backup by using DISKCOPY, and then work
on the backup rather than on the original.

EDLIN

The EDLIN.EXE file is remarkably short, some 7356
bytes, making EDLIN one of the few text editors that
can be crammed on to an already overcrowded
floppy disk and used for creating, editing and saving
ASCII text on to disk. There are no restrictions about
how it can be used, though its main use in the past
was in creating files of commands in what is called
assembly language that can be transformed into MS-
DOS EXE or COM files. The important point to
remember is that EDLIN is a *line* editor, so that lines
are numbered and you work with these numbers in
order to decide what you want to do.

Starting a file

When you call up EDLIN to create or change a text
file, you can follow the name EDLIN with a space,
and then with the filename that you want to use. If
you have a text file on the disk, and you want to edit
it further, then you will use this filename following
EDLIN, and the file will be obtained and presented
ready for use, with the message:

End of input file

Remember that this can be done only if you have
EDLIN on the same disk as the file, or available on
a suitable path. If you fail to specify a filename, you
will get the message:

File name must be specified

– and when you use EDLIN with a filename, the
screen message is:

NEW FILE
*

with the asterisk acting, as it always does in EDLIN,
as a prompt meaning that a command can be

accepted. This is important, because when the asterisk shows, only a *command* can be entered, not text. A further pointer to the age of EDLIN is that there is no cursor to show where you are working on text.

There is a huge list of command letters, which are listed below. The list is rather intimidating, but you'll find that only a few of these command letters are used extensively, and some of them might never be useful to you. It's a good idea if you intend to use EDLIN extensively to make a copy of the most useful command letters. In the list, letters j and k (and in some cases, ■ and n are used to mean numbers that have to be typed as part of the command.

j	edit line j (next line if j omitted). Use . (full-stop) to edit current line.
jA	add j lines of text to end of current text (from file).
j,k,■,nC	copy lines j to k to line before ■, make n copies. If j, k and c are omitted, one copy of current line is made. If k is omitted, only line j is copied.
j,kD	delete line j to line k. Omitting j and j deletes current line, omitting k deletes line j only.
E	end the editing session, record file and return to DOS.
jI	insert lines following line j; current line if j omitted. To end insertion of text, type Ctrl-C. To insert control codes, such as ESC, type Ctrl-V, then control character key.
j,kL	list lines j to k. If numbers are omitted, displays 23 lines starting at 11 lines before current line.
j,k,■M	move lines j to k to just before line ■.
j,kP	display lines j to k in sets of 23.
Q	quit edit, return to DOS without saving files. You will be asked to confirm this intention.
j,kR	search and replace. The command is followed by the

	string to be searched for, terminated with Ctrl-Z, then the string to replace it. If no replacement is provided, the old string will be deleted wherever it occurs. If the ? character is placed immediately before R, then confirmation will be required before each replacement.
j,kS	search lines j to k for string that is typed following S. If j is omitted, the search starts at the line following the current line. If k is omitted, the search is to the end of the file. Using ? just before S makes confirmation required for each find.
jT	followed by a filename will transfer that file into EDLIN immediately before line j. If j is omitted, the current line is used.
jW	write j lines to disk. If no number is specified, ¾ of the lines are written.

In addition, EDLIN uses its line numbers along with the symbols +, -, . and #. Typing +5 means choosing a line that is five lines further on from the current line, and -5 means five lines back. The . symbol means the current line, and # means the last line. Letter commands can be in upper or lower case, but uppercase has been used here in order to highlight the commands.

Insert text

When you are trying to create a file for the first time, the most useful command is I (Insert text). When you press I and then RETURN, the * display is replaced by 1:*, meaning that EDLIN is waiting for a line of text which will be numbered as line 1. This difference is *very* important, because when the number/colon/asterisk prompt is on a screen line, you can't issue command letters, and when the asterisk alone is on a screen line you can't type text. You can switch to the command mode (asterisk) by pressing Ctrl-C or Ctrl-Break, and return to the text mode by using I RETURN.

When you insert text, whether into a new blank file or into an existing file, you can type both upper and lower-case letters, by the normal use of the SHIFT key, in the numbered lines. You can therefore type whatever text you want, using RETURN to take a new line. The lines will be automatically numbered, but these numbers are *not* recorded with the file, and are an essential guide because all lines are referred to by number. When you use I with text already in the memory the remaining lines will be renumbered. Each time you alter the number of lines by inserting, replacing or deleting, the lines will be renumbered.

Editing

To edit text as you type, you can use the F1 to F5 keys as listed below, along with the DEL key, and the right or left arrow keys. Amstrad users should note that the Del-right and Del-left keys do *not* delete text in EDLIN, they will only cause the (invisible) cursor to move along the line. Unlike later editors, you do a lot of editing on a line which is initially invisible, with a complete copy just above it for reference purposes, as illustrated in this example:

```
6:* This is a test line
6:* This is
```

in which the word not is about to be inserted between is and a. Ins is pressed to allow inserting, and pressed again to stop inserting. With no cursor, the complete line is your only guide to where about on the line you are working.

Key	Use
F1	move along line one character at a time.
F2	copy the line up to a specified character.
F3	copy whole of line
F4	delete to specified character, follow with F3
F5	make new version of a line just after typing (before RETURN)

Example
```
0:*This is the line to be altered.
```

```
10:*
```
– at this point, press F2, then 0 keys
```
10:*This is the line t
```
– at this point press Insert and type on
```
10:*This is the line that is to be altered.
```
– now press RETURN to make this the current line for this number.

Example
```
12:*This is another line to be edited
12:*
```
– at this point type another replacement line
```
12:*A replacement line
```

– at this point type F5
```
12:*A replacement line
@
```

– at this point, you can edit your replacement line, which has not yet replaced the original line in memory.

```
12:*A replacement line
@A replacement type of line
```

– now press RETURN to make this the current line number 12

Once you appreciate what the character pointer of EDLIN is doing, the action of EDLIN becomes a lot easier to understand, if not easier to bear. Unlike modern word-processors, what you see may not be what you get, and what you do get you don't see right away. Despite all that, EDLIN is packed with features, not all of which you get on some high-cost programs. As you might expect, you can use EDLIN to find the position of anything in its text. Any search will start from the character pointer position, so if you want to search through the whole text, you have to start with the 1,S command.

Search and replace

For example, if you wanted to find the position of the word editor you could command 1,Seditor, with the 1 getting to the start of text, no number following the comma so that the last line is implied for the end of the search, and the word we are looking for, 'editor'. You have to be careful to type the word just as you expect to find it – if you specify 'editor', then you won't find 'Editor'.

When the command is executed, you'll see the whole line appear, and the usual single asterisk prompt. You can then use F3 to repeat the command, then RETURN to execute the command again, or you can type the line number so as to edit the line.

Suppose you want to carry out a search and replace action. The command letter for this is R and it has to be followed by the word you want to replace, then a `Ctrl-Z`, and then the word you want as a replacement. For example, suppose you wanted to replace 'text' by 'words', searching from lines 1 to 50, you would type:

`1,50Rtext^Zwords`

(`Ctrl-Z` shows on screen as `^Z`) and this would result in replacing each *text* in the file by *words*, ending the search at line 50. The line in which the search ended would be marked by an asterisk following the line number and colon. This line could be selected for editing by pressing the full-stop, then the RETURN key.

Any work that might need search and replace actions, however, is better carried out by a more modern editor, such as can be supplied as a public-domain program at low cost, or at reasonable prices commercially. Some full-blown word-processors are also very useful editors, and if you have a copy of PC-WRITE (formerly a shareware program) or WordStar Professional 4, then there is absolutely no need to use EDLIN.

DEBUG

Of the programmer's utilities on the MS-DOS System disk, the one that you are most likely to need at times is called DEBUG. In programmer's language, a bug is a fault in a program, debugging is removing bugs, and the cause of the bug is called, of course, a programmer. Using DEBUG definitely requires some knowledge about the machine and how it is designed, which is why it isn't a utility that you can use as you would use DIR, COPY or DEL. When DEBUG is loaded and run, it loads into the machine, using the lowest part of memory that is available.

The memory of the PC type of machine is specified in the form of two numbers which are combined to make an address number, and each address number that can be formed in this way corresponds to an address at which one byte will be stored. Since the PC is a 16-bit machine, many of the commands make use of two bytes at a time, and the address numbers are changed in twos.

The standard form of address is written in the form:

2F65 : 0100

using hexadecimal (hex) notation. If you need a reminder on hex notation, see Appendix A. The address consists of two numbers, the first of which 2F65 is stored in a Code Segment (CS) register of the microprocessor, while the other is stored in the Instruction Pointer (IP).

Many references to memory make use of the address numbers in this form, but the true address has to be calculated from this. The method is to add a zero to the end of the first number and then add the second, remembering that this is hexadecimal addition:

```
2F650
 0100
2F750
```

– so making the actual address 2F750H, where the H is a reminder that this is a hex number. This number corresponds to the denary number 194,384.

This is fairly typical of the address number range that you will find when DEBUG has been loaded. The memory starts at address zero, but it has been filled, as the machine started up, with the hidden files, part of COMMAND.COM, any SYS files that are used in CONFIG.SYS, and to this we have added DEBUG, so that it is hardly surprising that some 194,384 bytes have been used up out of the total, in a 640K machine, of 655360 bytes.

Note that this address could just as easily have been specified as:

2F75 : 0000

or as

2000 : F750

because this would give the same final result. The reason that the figure 0100 so often occurs is that all COM programs start with 0100 as the value in the IP register. The way that the designers of the microprocessor interpreted these numbers was to use the CS number (the first one) to contain a number which is the number of 64K segments (memory blocks), followed by zeros.

If this first number were 3000, for example, this would mean segment 3, if it were F0000 this would mean segment F (16 in normal numbering). By convention, a COM type of file starts at a number which is 0100 (hex) bites into a segment, so that a COM program located in segment 3 would start at address 30100. The EXE type of file can start at any number, because it is constructed in a way that allows the file to be relocated as it is being read into memory.

The reason for using this type of reference to memory is that it allows a 20-bit number (five hex digits) to be stored in two 16-bit registers. The snag is that when a program like DEBUG is used, it will split a memory address number up rather arbitrarily, so that the start of the program that is loaded following DEBUG has 0100 as its second number of the pair. You will quite often find that this has been done, and it tends to conceal the true segment number from you. This, however, does not prevent you from using DEBUG to get to any part of the memory that you choose.

For many purposes, however, there is no need to specify addresses in this split number way, because you will very often only be working with addresses in one single segment, a *relative address*, so that the address that is of interest will be the second number, the number in the IP register. This is particularly true when you are using DEBUG, as you normally are, to sort out some feature of a file. When you load DEBUG, you can specify also that the file that you want to work on will be loaded with it. For example, you can type DEBUG b:rped.exe so as to load in DEBUG, and also load in the program rped for DEBUG to work on. You would do this only if you were a programmer wanting to check or alter some part of the rped program, and if you are not a programmer it's more likely that you will not want to load in a file along with DEBUG, or if you do, it will be a modified text or other unusual ASCII file. There would be no point in using DEBUG to work on an ordinary text file, because any editor could do that, but if you wanted to alter a character in a text file to be a control character, for example, DEBUG is ideal. Working on program files definitely requires knowledge of the program, even if you are only going to alter a message on the screen to indicate that the program is your own property.

You may have found, however, advice in a magazine which shows you how to improve the action of a program by modifying part of the file, and you can use DEBUG to carry out this modification, and then save the modified version back to the disk (but *only* if you have another backup copy of the original). If, as is also likely, you want to use DEBUG only for investigating the contents of the memory of the PC, then all you need do is type DEBUG and press the RETURN key in the usual way.

Using DEBUG

Note: Where a number that is shown stored in the memory is composed of several bytes, these bytes are stored *in reverse order*. The number 2B7F, for example, would be stored in the order 7F 2B, because this is more convenient for the microprocessor to work with (in an addition, for example, the lower bytes are added first so that any carry can be added to higher bytes).

Once DEBUG is up and running, all you see to remind you is a 'prompt' that consists of a hyphen, -. When you see this reminder, you can give a command to DEBUG, consisting of a single letter (upper-case or lower-case) followed by pressing the RETURN key. The letter commands that can be used are listed here.

A	write in a simplified assembler language.
C	compare two blocks of memory for mismatch.
D	Dump memory. Show contents of 128 addresses in sequence.
E	enter codes into memory directly.
F	fill a block of memory with one byte repeated.
G	execute a program at stated address. Breakpoints can be set at which the execution will stop.
H	shows sum and difference of two hex numbers.
I	input one byte from a specified

	port.
L	Load, will load the file whose name has been typed in, see N. The filename can also be specified when DEBUG is entered. Another form of Load will load specified sectors directly from the disk
M	move a block of data to a new starting address.
N	Name, specifies the name of a file to be loaded or saved. The full name, including extension, must be used. This allows a filename to be changed if necessary.
O	output a byte from a specified port.
Q	leave (quit) debug, return to MS-DOS.
R	register display, showing the contents of the CPU registers.
S	Search for a pattern of numbers of characters.
T	trace instructions one at a time, showing the register contents at each step. The number of instructions per step can be altered.
U	unassemble code, converting hex code into assembler language instructions (whether these make sense or not).
W	write a named (with N) file (not a HEX or EXE file).

Memory Dump

From this list, you will see that the command that is most likely to be immediately useful is D, the memory dump command. A memory dump is a listing of each address in memory with the value of the code number that is stored in that byte. Obviously, a listing of the whole memory in this way would be impossibly large, because the PC can use over a million memory addresses, though only 655360 are available to be used for programs on the standard PC model, and this allocation includes all of the system files. After a dump has been displayed, you can display another, or use any of the other commands, including Q to leave DEBUG.

The dump command therefore displays in pages, consisting of 128 bytes of data at a time. The big problem is how to find what you are looking for. If you have loaded DEBUG along with a file, the second number of the two used to set an address will be set so that it corresponds to the start of the file. For a file with a .COM extension, for example, the second address number will normally be 0100, which in hex does not mean one hundred but 256. If you have loaded DEBUG on its own, the number also starts off at 0100, and to read any data in the memory, you either have to reset it, or use D and keep pressing keys (any key) to display another 128 byte section until you get to whatever you want.

In the example shown in Figure 7.1, DEBUG has been loaded and followed by a simple batch file, rather than a program file, so that it is easier to see the form of the display.

Note the high value of the CS register number, the first half of the address that indicates the start of each line. This is because DEBUG and the batch file were loaded in following the word-processor which was being used to write this chapter. WordStar allows you to make a temporary exit from word-processing to run other commands, and then return. The other commands were DEBUG C:WS.BAT > DB1.DOC (so that the results of DEBUG were dumped to a file that WordStar could then read), and when this had loaded, d for Dump and the q for Quit. No prompt is visible when the file is being redirected in this way, and the letters d and q are not visible either, so you need to know what you are doing if you use DEBUG in this fashion.

In this example, using D again will dump the next 256 bytes of data, but you might want to dump an entirely different part of the memory. This is done by specifying the address in the D command in more detail. If you are working in the same segment (first address number unchanged) you can use, for example, D 0150. If you want to move to an entirely different part of the memory, you can use D with a two-part address, such as D 2000:0100.

The listing shows the second address number set to the conventional 0100, and the next 16 columns display the bytes of the file, with the hyphen

```
7861:0100  65 63 68 6F 20 6F 66 66-0D 0A 63 64 20 63 3A 5C   echo off..cd c:\
7861:0110  77 73 74 61 72 20 0D 0A 77-73 0D 0A 65 63 68 6F   wstar..ws..echo
7861:0120  57 61 6E 74 20 74 6F 20-73 61 76 65 20 74 65 78   Want to save tex
7861:0130  74 20 74 6F 20 41 3A 20-3F 0D 0A 79 6E 0D 0A 69   t to A: ?..yn..i
7861:0140  66 20 65 72 72 6F 72 6C-65 76 65 6C 20 31 20 67   f errorlevel 1 g
7861:0150  6F 74 6F 20 67 65 74 6F-75 74 0D 0A 63 6F 70 79   oto getout..copy
7861:0160  20 2A 2E 74 78 74 20 61-3A 0D 0A 3A 67 65 74 6F    *.txt a:..:geto
7861:0170  75 74 0D 0A 63 64 20 63-3A 5C 0D 0A 64 69 72 20   ut..cd c:\.dir
-q
```

Figure 7.1

separating sets of eight. The ASCII codes for these bytes are shown in the right hand side of the file, but only where the ASCII code is between 32 and 127 inclusive. The hex codes 0A and 0D are the line feed and carriage return, respectively. Not shown here is the end of file byte, which is 1A, denary 26, the Ctrl-Z character.

Position in memory

Whether DEBUG is operating on a file that has been left at the bottom end of the memory because of a problem with some other program, or is working on a file that was loaded along with DEBUG, the DEBUG program will normally be automatically loaded into the lowest part of the memory that is free. This is what makes DEBUG so very convenient as a rescue program. If, for example, your word-processor crashes so that the DOS prompt re-appears on the screen, any attempt to reload the word processor to recover text will wipe the text out of the memory. If you load DEBUG, however, it will invariably take much less space than a word-processor, and it can be used to search through the memory until the text is found, then it can be used to save a file of the text, specifying the addresses of the start and the end of the text.

If a file is specified to be loaded along with DEBUG, the file is then loaded into the next available part of memory above DEBUG. This is normal for MS-DOS, which can arrange for programs to load in where they can run, but allowing other programs also to load and run. Either way, the data that you are working on will be in the memory addresses that it normally occupies. This allows us to do things like altering the codes in the memory, and saving the altered copy. This is one way of making a 'custom' copy of a program for our own purposes, but it is definitely not for the beginner or the user who feels that backing-up disks is a waste of time. You must never attempt any of these actions on any file or disk for which you do not have an adequate backup, preferably two backup copies.

Apart from the risk of losing a disk-full of data, there's nothing to prevent you from experimenting. It can't damage the computer, and if you lose a disk for which you have a couple of back-ups, then all you have really lost is time. On the other hand, you may very well have achieved something very useful that allows you to obtain considerably more from the computer in the future.

A printer file

This example illustrates DEBUG being used to produce a file that when printed using PRINT or TYPE (with CTRL-P), will set an Epson RX or FX printer into bold face. This is done by sending the ASCII codes 27 and 69 (code for letter E) to the printer, in that sequence. At first sight this looks very simple, and all you have to do is create a file with these characters. The problem is that, as we have seen, very few file editors will allow you to enter the ASCII Esc code which is 27. The solution is to enter some dummy value, and then use DEBUG to change the file.

Start by calling up your text editor (RPED for Amstrad users), specify a new file and name it BOLPRT, then make a file that consists only of a space and the letter E, whose ASCII code is 69. Now proceed as follows:

1 Enter DEBUG, using your filename. For example, use DEBUG b : BOLPRN if the printer file is on drive B.

2 Type d RETURN to see the file displayed. It should read: 20 45 0D 0A 1A 20 .. – with the rest of the file giving the 20 character code, which is the space.

3 The character 45 is E in ASCII code. This is 45 and not 69, because DEBUG *always* uses hexadecimal codes.

4 Type e100 RETURN. You will now see the number 20 displayed with a dot following it.

5 Type 1B and press the spacebar. This has the effect of changing the 20 number to 1B, the Esc code. Now press RETURN.

6 Press d100 RETURN to check that the change has been made.

7 Type w RETURN. This will return the file to the disk in its altered form, using the same filename.

8 Type q RETURN. This gets you out of DEBUG and back to the normal DOS prompt.

If you have an Epson printer on line, you can now test the BOLPRT file. Switch the printer on, and select a short file, such as a batch file like AUTOEXEC.BAT. Type

```
TYPE AUTOEXEC.BAT
```

press Ctrl-P, and then RETURN. The printer should print out the file in ordinary type. Press Ctrl-P again.

Now type:

```
TYPE BOLPRT
```

– press Ctrl-P, and then RETURN. The printer will take a new line, but probably won't print anything. Press Ctrl-P again, and try printing the AUTOEXEC.BAT file again. This time it should be in bold type, indicating that your BOLPRT file did as it was supposed to.

Your printer manual will show details of all the codes that alter printer behaviour. Many of these will start with the Esc character, which is 1B in hex. code, so that you can write a string of codes in this way to set up whatever you want. The general method that has been illustrated here will work just as well for any sequence of codes. You create a file with an editor, and use a space or an unusual character (such as `.`) for any character that you cannot enter, such as Esc. By using DEBUG with this file, you can then substitute these characters, and save the amended file. This file can then be printed as part of an AUTOEXEC.BAT sequence if you want your printer always set in this way, using the TYPE command in the AUTOEXEC.BAT file.

Floppy disk diagnosis

One particularly useful feature of DEBUG allows sectors of data stored on a disk to be loaded into the memory of the computer. This is one way in which data from a disk that has been damaged can be recovered, and it is the basis of the way in which a deleted file can be replaced. The problems of recovering a corrupted program file need very considerable knowledge of the system and of the program, but we can look in outline at how to recover deleted text files (ASCII files).

The trouble with this command, a variety of the Load command, is that it is never easy to work with, certainly not so easy as the disk utility programs that are sold specifically for the purpose. If you are concerned with the recovery of files from a hard disk, then a utility specifically designed for the purpose will be easier to use, though DEBUG can often prove to be more effective, given sufficient time. What follows, then, is a very brief description which is intended to be the basis for experiment rather than a do-it-yourself guide to any kind of file recovery from a damaged disk or deleted file.

To start with, the sectors on the disk are numbered starting with 0 and going up to 719. In hex, this latter number is 02CF. The number is not quite so straightforward as you might think, however, because of the way that the double-sided disks are used. Sector 0 is on the first side of the disk, and is the first sector of the first track. There are 9 sectors on each track, so that the numbering of sectors goes from 0 through 1, 2, 3..up to sector 8, which is the last sector (since we started at 0) on Track 0, first side. The count then continues, but sector 9 is the first sector of Track 0 on the other side of the disk, and in this track we find sectors 9 to 17. Sectors 18 to 26 are on Track 1 on the first side, and sectors 27 to 35 on Track 1 of the second side and so on. The loading direct from sectors depends on making use of these numbers, but in the hex scale. The best way to experiment is on a copy of a disk that has been formatted with no System tracks, and has been used only for text.

The L command of DEBUG, when it is used for loading disk sectors, requires *four* numbers following it, all in hex. The first number is a starting number in memory, and a good choice is the usual 0100. The next number is 0 for Drive A, 1 for drive B, 3 for drive C or 4 for drive D. The third number is a starting sector number. DEBUG numbers sectors starting with the first sector of track zero, side 1, and the count moves to track 0 side 2, then back to track 1 side 0 and so on. For a disk of text, a good choice is 0C, because this is sector 12, the first one that is likely to be used. Sectors up to this are kept clear in case you want to add the system tracks. The fourth number is the number of sectors that you want to read. You can try 10 which is sixteen sectors (10 hex is 16 in normal numbering).

With DEBUG running, type:

```
L 100 0 C 10 RETURN
```

– and the disk will spin briefly, leaving you with the DEBUG prompt again. Now type:

D 100 RETURN

and you will see the start of the text on the disk. You can now alter the text, using E as in the example earlier. For a text disk, this is hardly worthwhile, because you could do the same with less hassle by using an editor. The point, however, is to show that DEBUG can deal with anything, and that includes items that text editors cannot deal with, like the Esc character, and files that are on a disk and which might be corrupted. The file can be put back on the disk in its altered form by using the W command. If, for example, you use DEBUG to replace one character in a file with the number 1AH, which is the end-of-file marker, the file can from then on only be read as far as this point. If a file cannot be read correctly by a text editor, it may be that some disk corruption has placed the 1A character on the disk at an unwanted point, and that you could find it and remove it.

Register inspection

Register inspection with DEBUG makes use of the R command when DEBUG is working with a file loaded, or with its address changed to some part of the memory. The command is useful only if you have some experience of assembly language programming so that you know what the registers ought to be showing. The display is of the form:

```
-r
AX=0000 BX=0000 CX=5C3C DX=0000 SP=FFFE BP=0000 SI=0000
DI=0000 DS=787A ES=787A SS=787A CS=787A IP=0100 NV UP EI PL NZ NA PO NC
787A:0100 E9DD0B   JMP   0CE0
-q
```

– which shows the content of each register at the address which is given at the start of the third line. Note that this address corresponds, as it ought to, with the contents of the CS and IP registers. This is a COM type of file which is being debugged, so that the starting address with 0100 in the IP register is genuine. The SP register shows the stack pointer at FFFE, the normal starting position before a program starts. There is a word of data in the CX register, but none in any of the other general-purpose registers, AX, BX and DX. The two index registers SI and DI are set to zero, as also is the base pointer BP.

The flag line shows the state of the flags which report the results of the action. Eight of nine flags are shown here, using two-letter codes to indicate the settings. The meanings of all possible two-letter reports (two for each flag) are:

OV	Overflow occurred
NV	No overflow
DN	Direction down (decrement)
UP	Direction up (increment)
EI	Enable interrupt
DI	Disable interrupt
NG	Result negative
PL	Result positive
ZR	Result zero
NZ	Result not zero
AC	Auxiliary carry made
NA	No auxiliary carry
PE	Parity even
PO	Parity odd
CY	Carry took place
NC	No carry

In the example, there is no overflow, and the direction flag shows UP (it usually does, and its setting is not used in any tests). The direction flag is used in connection with the index registers to show whether the register is being incremented (UP) or decremented (DN). Interrupts are enabled, and the command that has just been executed left a positive result, not zero. There was no auxiliary carry, parity is odd, and no carry was generated.

The left hand side of the last line in the register display shows the instruction that has been read from memory starting at the current address. This shows that at the address 787A : 0100 the command in hex code was E9DD0B, a three-byte command, meaning JMP 0CE0. This assumes, as it always does, that the codes are genuine command codes and not simply stored data, because there is no simple way of distinguishing between the two if they are mixed up together. The address 0CE0 is obtained by adding the address to which the program would normally go next (0103) to the displacement number shown in the JMP command (0BDD, written in reverse order as

DD0B), because 0103 + 0BDD = 0CE0. The alternative use of the R command is in modifying a register.

Example
R AX 0300

– will place the word 0300 into the AX register. To see that this has been carried out, you need to make use of R by itself again. Modification of registers can be used to change the IP number so as to look at another address. In the previous example, the jump to 0CE0 can be followed by using:

R IP 0CE0

– which will change the content of IP to this address and allow whatever is stored at this address to be viewed by using R or D.

Searching through memory

The S command allow the memory to be searched for a specified byte or group of bytes or for a string of characters. If the search is for a byte, then that byte can be specified in hex; for a group of bytes, the bytes are separated by spaces. When a string is to be searched for, it can be specified as character rather than as ASCII codes, such as 'BAT'.

A search will be made specifying a start address and an ending address, because it would be time-wasting to search all the way through memory. The addresses can be specified in three ways, following a pattern similar to the D command:

1 As an address in the current segment like CS:1CE4 (or just 1CE4)
2 As a complete address like 3000:1050
3 For the second number only, as a length like L200

– the length number uses the letter L to distinguish it from an address, and the number of bytes that follows the L is in hex.

Example
D F000:C0000 L60 'plc'

– will give the result F000:C033 which will be the address of this message, the start of the Resident Operating System (ROS) of the Amstrad PC, and a dump of this part of the memory, given in Figure 7.2, shows that the search action was correct

```
F000:C000  E9 D7 00 28 43 29 20 43-6F 70 79 72 69 67 68 74  ..(C) Copyright
F000:C010  20 31 39 38 36 20 41 6D-73 74 72 61 64 20 43 6F   1986 Amstrad Co
F000:C020  6E 73 75 6D 65 72 20 45-6C 65 63 74 72 6F 6E 69   nsumer Electroni
F000:C030  63 73 20 70 6C 63 28 28-43 29 29 20 20 43 43 43   cs plc((CC))  CC
F000:C040  6F 6F 70 70 79 79 72 72-69 69 67 67 68 68 74 74   ooppyyrriigghhtt
F000:C050  20 20 31 31 39 39 38 38-36 36 20 20 41 41 6D 6D   1199886 AAmm
F000:C060  73 73 74 74 72 72 61 61-64 64 20 20 43 43 6F 6F   ssttrraadd CCoo
F000:C070  6E 6E 73 73 75 75 6D 6D-65 65 72 72 20 20 45 45   nnssuummeerr EE
```

-q

Figure 7.2

An alternative would have been to type the search command as:

```
S F000:C000 C07F 70 6C 63
```

– using the absolute address for the first address, a relative address (IP register number) for the second, and the ASCII codes in hex for the required bytes. For searching through machine-code program files in which a set of instruction codes rather than a recognisable name is wanted, this second form is better, and can be used with all of the usual address methods, or with L marking the number of bytes which are to be searched.

Example

```
DEBUG COMMAND.COM
-S CS:0100 9000 A8 01 B0 01 74 02 B0 05
```

– will find where this set of bytes is stored in COMMAND.COM. Then by changing the B0 01 to B0 02, the DIR display of the computer is changed to double-column (and DIR/W to four column). If you specify only a few bytes in a search, there is a chance that the combination will occur several times. If this happens, DEBUG will print a list of addresses, and you may want to redirect this list to a file or to the printer in order to make reference to it later.

The C command exists so that two blocks of memory can be compared, byte by byte, and any differences noted. The form of the display is to show only where differences exist, in the form of first address, byte, second byte, second address. The C command is followed by the starting address of the first memory block, then the number of bytes (using L to indicate length), then the starting address for the second block of memory. As usual, if the full address is not given, the number is assumed to be in the current segment.

Example

```
C 0200 L20 0300
```

– will compare 20H bytes (32 bytes) starting at 0200 in the current segment with the 20H bytes starting at address 0300 in the same segment. If these bytes were identical except for the corresponding addresses 021A and 031A, then the display would be:

```
2F65:021A 1A 3C 2F65:031A
```

– with the code segment being 2F65 in this example.

Changing memory

While DEBUG is working on any part of the memory, including a program file stored in the memory, it can use the codes E and F to alter memory contents. The E command means enter into memory, and has to be followed by an address number of a point where you want to start making alterations. As usual, this address can be given in the forms:

0115	a position in the current segment
CS:0115	also in current segment
3000:0115	the full address

and when the RETURN key is used, you will be shown the (full) address followed by the byte which is stored at that address and a full-stop, which is the entry prompt. You can then either:

– enter a new byte, as two hex characters, *or*

– press the space-bar to leave the byte unchanged.

and you will then see the next existing byte appear. Do *not* press RETURN, as this terminates the action. If you have altered a byte, you will see that byte, the full-stop and your alteration, followed by the next byte in the sequence. To edit an incorrect entry (before pressing RETURN), press the hyphen key. To end the entry of data, press RETURN without entering any data. The example is illustrated with a batch file for simplicity, but the E command would always be used for altering program files.

Example
```
DEBUG WS.BAT
-e 0100
6AF1:0100 65.68 63.64 68.
-q
```

– which has changed the start of the file, the word echo to hdho. The important point is that changes could just as easily be made to the file COMMAND.COM (try the wide-directory modification as outlined in the S command) or to any other file that you use. *Never* attempt such changes unless you have a backup of the file on another disk.

The F command will fill an area of memory with a byte or set of bytes, and the byte that is used is generally 00, since this is a way of indicating that the memory is cleared. Though the command does not have many uses, it is indispensable for the task it does, since no-one would want to use the E command to enter 8K of zeros into a block of memory. The fill character need not be a single byte, however, but can be a set such as 'ABCDEFGH', distinguished by the use of the single (or double) quote character at each end of the string. The start and stop addresses, or a start address and a length, must be specified, followed by the byte or string.

Example
F 0100 2FFF 0

– will fill from 0100 to 2FFF in the current segment with the byte 0.

Example
F 0000 L 500 'ABCD'

– will fill memory in the current segment from 0000, for 500H bytes (1280 bytes) with the repeating string ABCD.

The M command copies a set of bytes from one part of the memory to another, and can be used to make a copy in RAM of data that is normally held in the ROM. The starting address of the data and its ending address or length must be specified, followed by the starting address of the part of memory where the data is to be copied. As usual, if only a single address number is given, the current segment is assumed, but addresses can also be shown in full, either as numbers or in the form register:number. For example, if the ES register stores the number 3000H, then an address of ES:0100 is equivalent to an address of 3000:0100.

Example
M 0100 L4F 1FC4

– will move 4F bytes (79 bytes) starting at 0100 in the current segment to an address starting at 1FC4 in the same segment.

Example
M 2000:0100 L1000 ES:0100

– will move 1000H bytes (4096 bytes) starting at address 2000:0100 and shift them to an address ES:0100, whose exact value depends on whatever number is stored in the ES register at the time.

Inputs and outputs

The specialised use of the L command for loading disk sectors, and W for writing the sectors back to disk has already been noted. These forms of the commands are used for inspecting disk contents as distinct from file contents, so that the inputs and outputs referred to here are for files and ports. Very often, the only way that you will need to get a file inspected by DEBUG is by typing the name of the file following the DEBUG name. The alternative is to enter DEBUG, and then use the Name command to enter a name for loading or saving. You can, of course, load a file under one name and then alter the name before saving again.

The N command is used only for naming a file and it has no visible effect. Once it has been used, however, the load and save commands will make use of that filename but with an important exception. Though you can *read* a file whose extension is .HEX or .EXE, you are *not permitted* to write a file with these extension names. If you need to read such a file, alter it and write it back, then you will have to change the name by using the normal REN command of MS-DOS before and after using DEBUG (an extension such as .BIT can be used). The N command can be used after a file has been loaded in order to name any other files that will be loaded when that file is run. If, to take an example, you have a program RESTFILE.COM which can read and modify another file MYTXT.TXT, then you can load in DEBUG, load in the file RESTFILE.COM and then use N to name the file MYTXT.TXT. If the RESTFILE program is then run using DEBUG to inspect what happens during running (see later), then it will load MYTXT.TXT when it comes to the appropriate stage.

The form of the N command is simply the letter followed by a space and then the name. The extension letters for the file *must* be included, unless there is no extension.

Example
```
Nspoolit.com
```

– sets up the filename in the memory ready for loading or saving actions.

The L command will load a file whose name has been established using the N command. Precisely where in the memory the file is loaded depends on the type of the file, and for some types of file there will be a choice of address. If the file extension is COM, then the file will be loaded so that the first instruction in the file will be placed at the relative address of 0100 hex, with the segment address placed in the CS register in the usual way. The BX and CX registers are used to hold the number of bytes that have actually been loaded into memory. This will be equal to file length for a COM type of file, with the BX register holding the fifth hex digit for a long file. For the EXE type of file, the starting address will have been held as part of the file and will not normally be 0100. In addition, the number of bytes that have been loaded (in the BX:CX registers) will be *less* than the file length. This is because the file holds data about how to make alterations in order that the file can be located starting at any specified memory location, and these relocation bytes need not be kept when the file has been loaded.

When the file is a text file, or any file which is not of the COM or EXE type (or the HEX type, an intermediate between assembly language and COM or EXE), you can use the L command along with an address (full or relative) to force the file to be stored starting at this address. The BX and CX registers will be set to show the length of the file, and the segment that is used will be the segment that corresponds to an address 100H bytes *before* the start of the file (following the same convention about COM and EXE files starting at 0100H). Remember that if you have loaded a file to some address other than CS:0100 that the D command will still display the bytes starting at CS:0100 unless you specify otherwise.

Example
N MYFIL.COM
L

– will load in this file at the lowest available address, with the relative displacement of *0100*. The length of the file is equal to the number of bytes loaded and is shown in the BX:CX registers – for most practical purposes, this means the CX register alone.

Example
N MYFIL.EXE

L

– will load in the file at the lowest possible address and show the starting address in the CS:IP registers. The IP register number will *not* be 0100, and the number in the BX:CX register pair will not be as large as the size of the file as indicated in the DIR display.

Example

N MYFIL.DOC

L 0000

– will load the file at relative address 0000 in whatever segment is available at relative address FF00 (100H bytes before 0000).

The W command allows a file that is being worked on by DEBUG to be written back to the disk. In most ways, the W command is the opposite of the L command, and this includes the writing of disk sectors, but the important exception is that a file of the EXE (or HEX) type cannot be written unless its extension has been changed before loading. The amount of data that will be written is specified by the number in the BX:CX register pair, and the starting address will be CS:0100 unless another address is specified (which is why EXE files are excluded, because unless they are renamed, they will not load to CS:0100 and cannot be correctly saved from that address).

Example

W

– will write the file, using the filename specified by the N command, from addresses starting at CS:0100, and for a number of bytes specified by BX:CX.

The I and O commands are more specialised, and deal with the input and output ports. These ports are used to allow the computer to read in bytes from external sources (like serial input) and to send out bytes (to a loudspeaker, parallel printer, serial modem and so on). You cannot make use of the I and O commands unless you know the address numbers for the ports on your computer and how they are used. The standard port A, B and C address numbers are 060H, 061H and 062H, with serial ports at 03F8 to 03FF and parallel printer on 0378 to 037A, and for the use of these ports or details of other ports such as light-pen ports, you should consult the technical manual for your PC. Each bit is used for a different purpose, so that considerable care has to be taken when writing to a port (using the 0 command) that the correct bit is being changed.

The form of commands is that I is followed by an address, and 0 is followed by an address and a byte.

Example
```
I 062
23
```

– displays output from Port C indicating in this case that 640K RAM is installed, and that there is a timer bit present.

Example
```
0 061 01
```

– sends a 1 to the loudspeaker. If this command is use to send 0 and 1 alternately (in a loop) then a note will be sounded.

Go and Trace

The commands that display or alter the contents of file or memory are comparatively innocuous in the sense that though they can alter data they will not have any effect on the computer until the file is used. The G and T commands allow programs to be run under the control of DEBUG, and unless considerable care is taken, or the program is known to run without problems, it is possible that the computer could lock up. The G and T commands are normally used when testing a machine-code program that is suspected of being troublesome, so when these commands are to be used, backup copies must be made first of all. *Never* use G or T commands on a file that is not a program COM or EXE file.

The G command will start executing a program from any address and can allow up to ten stopping places (or *breakpoints*) to be specified. For a short program, or one which was though to be working normally, no breakpoints might be set and if the program ends normally, a message to this effect will be displayed. If another run is required the program will have to be reloaded first.

Example
```
G
Program terminated normally
```

– the program has run without problems and will have to be reloaded if another run is required. If the program has altered memory, then you can use the D command to check what has happened. Normal termination is no guarantee that the program has done what you expected it to do, only that it has ended without locking up the computer. If, as will certainly happen in the event of a fault in the program section or incorrect selection of starting point or breakpoint, the machine does lock up, you will have to restart. Make sure that you have backups of any files that might be affected, and always make a note of what you have done, so that you do not repeat mistakes.

When an address follows the G command, the execution will be forced to start from this address. When you start at the beginning of a program, there is no need to specify an address because this will be taken from the CS:IP registers, ensuring that the correct address is used for either a COM or an EXE file. The use of an address is a way of starting a program at some point other than the beginning, and requires you to know where suitable starting point are. Incorrect selection of a starting address will almost certainly cause a lock-up.

Example
G = 020C

– will start the program running at address CS:020C.

When an address is specified *without* the equality sign, this address is taken as being a breakpoint, a place where the program is forced to stop. In some programs, more than one breakpoint might have to be specified because there might be branching commands that could lead to any one of a number of addresses being used after a number of commands of the program have been executed. DEBUG allows up to 10 breakpoints to be entered, separated by spaces. Note that these do *not* imply that the program can be resumes after breaking at one point to be caught at another. Each time breakpoints are to be used, another G instruction must be typed along with whatever breakpoints are to be checked.

Example
G 3CF 5A2

– will start the program from its normal starting point (CS:IP address) and break at 3CFH or 5A2H, whichever is first used in the program. When the break occurs, the register contents will be displayed, and the DEBUG prompt, the hyphen, will appear to indicate that you can enter any valid DEBUG command. This allows you to resume, using G with an address following the breakpoint and specifying more breakpoints.

The use of T is a way of sorting out a small section of a program that is proving stubbornly troublesome. This command will trace what is happening, step by step, either one command for each T or a multiple, but whichever method is used, the full register contents will be shown for each step.

Example
T

– will execute the command at the address in the CS:IP registers, then display the register contents.

Example
T5

– will execute the first five commands, starting at the current CS__IP address, and displaying register contents at each step.

If the part of a program that is under investigation contains a loop, it is often better to use G with a breakpoint just following the loop, and the T to find out what happens next, rather than use T round each part of the loop in each run round the loop. You should *not* continue to use T to follow a call into MS-DOS or into the ROM BIOS.

Assembly and unassembly

The A and U commands of DEBUG allow for a very limited form of assembly language working. The A command permits assembly language to be written and placed in memory, but without any editing facilities, so that you cannot slip in an extra command between two others. The U command allows an existing program to be unassembled (or disassembled), showing the assembly language lines that correspond to the machine-code bytes. This assumes that all of the bytes are genuine code, because the U command cannot distinguish between ASCII coded text and machine code instructions.

Before the U command is used, then, the code should be looked at using the D command to see where the text, if any, has been placed. The address boundaries for the text should be noted, and these addresses not used along with the U command.

The A command permits *limited* assembly language facilities for very small-scale work only. The main limitations and differences are:

1 No address labels can be used, so that any reference to other positions in memory have to be made using the memory address.
2 No data labels can be used, so that bytes such as 0DH must be shown as such, and not as word labels like CR.
3 RET instructions must use RETF for a FAR return.
4 An address location is shown inside square brackets
5 MOVESB is used for moving a string byte into memory
6 MOVESW is used for moving a string word into memory.
7 The normal assembler use of a full address is modified so that in place of MOV AX,DS:012F, DEBUG uses DS:MOV AX,[012F]

The advantage of the A command is that it can be very quick to use for short routines, since no assembly time is needed – the code is placed directly into the memory. The form of the command is A followed by the starting address at which the code is to be written.

Example
```
A 0100
6AF1:0100 mov AH,02
6AF1:0102 mov DL,0f
6AF1:0104 int 21
6AF1:0106 int 20
6AF1:0108
-d 0100
6AF1:0100   B4 02 B2 0F CD 21 CD 20-00
```

– allows the lines of assembly language to be written, showing the full address for the first byte in each line. This does *not* show the actual bytes of assembly language, so that a D command has been used in this example, and only part of the first line is shown.

The U command allows for un-assembly of code, with the usual proviso that any bytes will be treated as code. If the start of the code is at the location given by the contents of CS:IP, then no address needs to be given in the U command, but normally both a starting address and a length (using L) will be specified. The result will be an assembly language version of the bytes in the memory, rather as they would be produced by the *A* command of DEBUG, with absolute memory addresses. If no length byte is specified, DEBUG will unassemble 20H (32 denary) bytes.

If ASCII text has been present, it will be interpreted as code, and the usual clues to this are jumps to impossible addresses, or the use of very rare and meaningless instructions. Similarly, if an unassembly is started at an address which is in fact the middle of an instruction, the results will be meaningless.

Example

```
DEBUG EXAMP.COM
-U cs:0100 L2B
6B09:0100 BA1801     MOV    DX,0118
6B09:0103 B8013D     MOV    AX,3D01
6B09:0106 CD21       INT    21
6B09:0108 93         XCHG   BX,AX
6B09:0109 BA1C01     MOV    DX,011C
6B09:010C B91000     MOV    CX,0010
6B09:010F B440       MOV    AH,40
6B09:0111 CD21       INT    21
6B09:0113 B8004C     MOV    AX,4C00
6B09:0116 CD21       INT    21
6B09:0118 50         PUSH   AX
6B09:0119 52         PUSH   DX
6B09:011A 4E         DEC    SI
6B09:011B 001B       ADD    [BP+DI],BL
6B09:011D 4D         DEC    BP
6B09:011E 1B471B     SBB    AX,[BX+1B]
6B09:0121 52         PUSH   DX
6B09:0122 031B       ADD    BX,[BP+DI]
6B09:0124 6C         DB     6C
6B09:0125 0A1B       OR     BL,[BP+DI]
6B09:0127 51         PUSH   CX
6B09:0128 5A         POP    DX
6B09:0129 1B4E02     SBB    CX,[BP+02]
-q
```

– has unassembled the bytes of a short program, treating all of the bytes as code. In this example, the

last 16 bytes are *not* program code but data to be sent
to a printer, and the bytes following address 0117
must be treated as dubious. The sequence 50 52 4E
when viewed with the D command gives PRN, the
name for printer output.

Finally, the H command allows hexadecimal
arithmetic to be performed while DEBUG is running,
and is a useful way of checking jump number and
other arithmetic. The H command is followed by two
numbers, and will print the sum and the difference
of these numbers, which can be of 1 to 4 hex digits.

Example
h 01f7 3cd6
3ECD C521
-q

– showing that the sum of the numbers is 3ECDH
and the difference (meaning 01F7 – 3CD6) is C521.

8 MS-DOS interactions

The use of MS-DOS to run programs has been covered in the first six chapters of this book, and the use of MS-DOS utilities to write text files and to debug machine-code programs has been dealt with in Chapter 7. What follows is for the programmer dealing with MS-DOS, designing or maintaining programs or additions to programs which make use of MS-DOS rather than using the ROM of the computer. By making use of MS-DOS, a program can be made to suit a range of different machines that run MS-DOS, as distinct from the need to write a different version of the program for each machine.

The most important of MS-DOS interactions are with assembly language, but many high-level languages make provision for direct calls to MS-DOS, and two examples are noted at the end of this chapter. Much software nowadays is written in a high-level language, often C or Pascal, but such programs are invariably considerably longer and slower-running than the equivalent written in assembly language. The operating speed of many programs written in a high level language can be greatly increased by identifying critical sections which can be written in assembly language, compiled to machine code and called as required from the high-level language.

The Interrupt system

The interaction of any computing language with the routines of the operating system, whether it is with the ROM BIOS or MS-DOS, is done through the interrupt system. An interrupt is an electrical signal which can be generated by hardware (such as by the presence of a signal at an input port) or by software (execution of one of the INT commands of assembly language). This signal is linked to a pin, one of two, on the microprocessor chip and the effect of the signal will be to interrupt whatever is being done in order to run another routine. The interruption is handled in a methodical way, with any current instruction being completed, all the relevant data such as next address and register contents saved temporarily in the memory, and the new routine taken from an address in memory that can be fixed or specified by the way that the interrupt is carried out.

The use of two interrupt pins allows for two forms of interrupts, the non-maskable and the maskable. The non-maskable interrupt (NMI) is used only when the cause of the interruption is something that cannot be dealt with by any software routine, such as a falling supply voltage or a failure of the memory. As the name suggests, this type of interrupt signal has an immediate effect that cannot be disabled (masked) by any software command. It is unlikely that anyone other than a circuit designer will have any use for this type of interrupt.

The other type of interrupt is maskable, meaning that the signal that appears on the pin need not have any effect until a software enabling signal exists in the form of an interrupt-enable flag in the flag register. When this flag is set (EI), then a signal to the interrupt pin can cause an interrupt. When this flag is reset (DI) no interrupt can take place. This makes it possible to avoid interrupts during processes that rely on maintaining strict timing, such as disk inputs and outputs.

The microprocessor recognises interrupts by checking the signal voltage at the interrupt pins at the end of each instruction that it carries out. If the EI flag is set and there is a signal on the maskable interrupt pin, a piece of program called the *interrupt service routine* is run. On the PC machines, the maskable interrupt to the microprocessor is handled through an intermediate chip, the programmable interrupt controller. This chip provides both the interrupt and the address of the interrupt service routine, and allows up to 256 different routines to be called by number. For each number of interrupt, there will be four bytes stored in memory in an *interrupt vector table*, and these bytes provide the address of each routine, stored so that they can be transferred to the CS and IP registers of the microprocessor.

The assembly language form of a numbered interrupt is INT n, where n is a number in the range 0 to 255 inclusive. When this is translated into machine code it appears, in hex, as the number code *CD* followed by the value of n in hex, so that CD 20 means interrupt number 32. It is more usual to keep to hex numbering for these interrupts, however.

Machine interrupts

The possible range of interrupts contains many which are reserved for calling in special circumstances, and which relate to the microprocessor rather than to the use of MS-DOS. The first set of interrupts, for example, with all numbers in hex, is as shown below, though the uses of interrupts 5 to 1F will vary from one machine to another:

INT 00	divide by zero error
INT 01	single step (used by DEBUG **T** command)
INT 02	non-maskable interrupt
INT 03	breakpoint interrupt (used by DEBUG)
INT 04	overflow in multiplication
INT 05	print screen (software interrupt)
INT 06	mouse button control (software interrupt)
INT 07	reserved software interrupt
INT 08	system clock
INT 09	keyboard
INT 0A	real time clock
INT 0B	Communications 1
INT 0C	Communications 2
INT 0D	hard disk
INT 0E	floppy disk
INT 0F	printer
INT 10	VDU (software interrupt)
INT 11	system configuration (software interrupt)
INT 12	memory size (software interrupt)
INT 13	disk input/output (software interrupt)
INT 14	serial input/output (software interrupt)
INT 15	reserved for enhancement (software interrupt)
INT 16	keyboard input/output (software interrupt)
INT 17	printer input/output (software interrupt)
INT 18	system restart (software interrupt)
INT 19	disk bootstrap (software interrupt)
INT 1A	system clock and real-time clock

	in/out (software interrupt)
INT 1B	keyboard break (software interrupt)
INT 1C	external timer interrupt (software interrupt)
INT 1D	initialize VDU parameter table (software interrupt)
INT 1E	disk parameter table (software interrupt)
INT 1F	matrix table for VDU (software interrupt)
INT 14-1F	reserved for use by future Intel chips, so that the use of these interrupts would make programs potentially incompatible. There are also two unofficial interrupt numbers, 28H and 29H.

MS-DOS interrupts

MS-DOS can make use of the interrupts 20H to 3FH which are reserved for MS-DOS use with the Intel chip set. Of these, the INT 21H is by far the most important, as this is the way in which virtually all of the common MS-DOS actions are called up. The use of INT 21 will therefore be dealt with in much more detail than the others which are noted in the table. Of these, some are reserved for future expansion, and it is important if programs are being written for a variety of machines that the set of actions which is used should be common to at least the versions of MS-DOS from 3.0 onwards. Though at the time of writing, MS-DOS has reached V4.1, the differences between 4.1 and 3.0 relate mainly to actions that will not concern the majority of programmers who are concerned with adapting programs or with writing short program sections. The maintenance of compatibility is more important than the ability to use advanced features, particularly since there will be machines using versions 3.0 to 3.2 for a considerable time to come. It is only comparatively recently that it has been possible to start ignoring the earlier versions 1.x and 2.x in writing new programs.

MS-DOS interrupts in detail

The MS-DOS interrupts contain several duplications of actions, many of them due to the evolution of MS-

DOS over the years. In the following table, the interrupts are described only in outline, and a full listing of the INT 21H set follows. The interrupts described as *Unofficial* are not documented by MS-DOS but have been explored by others and reported on. Their use is discouraged, since such uses could change from one version of DOS to another.

INT 20H	End of program. Seldom used now, because there is a better version in INT 21H.
INT 21H	The MS-DOS function interrupt which allow the use of the functions listed later.
INT 22H	End of program vector, the address to which the machine goes when a program ends.
INT 23H	Ctrl-Break address for the start of the routine that takes over when Ctrl-Break is pressed.
INT 24H	Critical error address for the start of the routine that takes over when a critical error occurs. These are: Write-protected disk, Unknown unit, Drive not ready Unknown command, Data error, Bad request structure length, Seek error, Unknown media, Sector not found, Printer out of paper, Write fault, Read fault, General failure.
INT 25H	Disk read of specified track/sectors.
INT 26H	Disk write of specified track/sectors.
INT 27H	Terminate and stay resident (older method).
INT 28H	Unofficial re-entry to DOS for TSR programs.
INT 29H	Unofficial character output.
INT 2AH-2EH	Reserved for future use.
INT 2FH	Time-sharing interrupt, used by PRINT.
INT 30H-3FH	Reserved for future use.

The INT 21 functions

A call to INT 21 is used to carry out an action of MS-DOS, and the call involves three steps-

1 A function number is placed in the AH register.
2 Other numbers, as required by the action, are placed in other registers of the microprocessor.
3 The INT 21 is executed.

Each of the functions is documented in such a way that the contents of the registers before and after the call can be determined. If registers are likely to be modified by a call, the programmer may need to save these registers on the stack in the usual way. The use of INT 21 is therefore very extensive, since as many functions can be catered for as there can be numbers stored in the AH register. The following list is in numerical order for ease of looking up rather than in the order of probable use, and describes the functions briefly. For a full description, consult a text of MS-DOS programming. Note that many functions relate to the File Control Block system which was used for file identification in the 1.x versions of MS-DOS, and are retained only for compatibility purposes. Use the system of File Handles (introduced with V.2.0) for all programs being written, unless there is a particular need to maintain compatibility with Versions prior to 2.0.

When a function is called, it may cause an error, and there has to be a provision for reporting the error. The method that is used is to set the carry flag if an error has occurred (clear otherwise) and to return an error number in the AX register. The error codes are noted later in this chapter.

Functions 00H to 2EH are used in all versions of MS-DOS. Functions 2FH to 57H are used in version 2.0 onwards, and functions 58H onwards are used in V3.0 onwards, though function 63H is used in V2.25 and in no other version. V.3.3 functions start at 65H, and functions from 69H start to appear on V4.x.

A few descriptions start with the word *unofficially*, meaning that the use is undocumented by Microsoft, and may be changed. Such functions should be avoided, and if they are found in software, they might need to be replaced.

Function 00H – used to terminate COM programs only.

Function 01H – read key, echo on screen. Character code is returned in AL register.

Function 02H – byte in DL register displayed on screen.

Function 03H – serial port input, byte in AL register.

Function 04H – serial port output, byte in DL register.

Function 05H – parallel printer output, byte in DL register.

Function 06H – keyboard input or screen output depending on value in DL register.

Function 07H – key input, no echo, character in AL register.

Function 08H – as 07H, but checks for Ctrl-Break.

Function 09H – print string whose address is in DS:DX. String end marked with $ which is not printed.

Function 0AH – key input, buffered. DS:DX set to start of buffer, of which first byte is a length byte, second byte will be set to number of characters, and string starts at third byte. Carriage return ends input, 'bell' sounds if buffer is filled. Editing keys can be used on buffered characters.

Function 0BH – check input. AL register contains FFH if any input character available, 00H otherwise.

Function 0CH – clear buffer and read. AL register must contain a read code, such as 01H. The keyboard buffer will be cleared, and a read carried out.

Function 0DH – clear disk buffers.

Function 0EH – drive select, using number in DL register. After use, AL contains number of drives (minimum 2 even on a single-drive machine).

Function 0FH – file open using file-control block (FCB) system (for compatibility with older versions). DS:DX set to address of the FCB, which must not already be open.

Function 10H – file close, update directory. DS:DX contains address of open FCB.

Function 11H – match filename, using FCB. DS:DX contains address of FCB, and the directory will be searched for the name in this FCB, which can contain wildcards. AL contains 00H if successful.

Function 12H – next match search, will continue the search started by function 11H.

Function 13H – file delete using FCB. DS:DX contains address of FCB.

Function 14H – read sequential file using FCB.

DS:DX contains address of open FCB, data is read into disk transfer address (see Function 1AH).

Function 15H – write sequential file using FCB. DS:Dx contains address of open FCB, which contains details of file to be written.

Function 16H – file create using FCB. DS:DX contains address of unopened FCB. Function checks directory for existing file, or free space.

Function 17H – file rename using FCB. DS:DX contains address of FCB.

Function 18H – reserved.

Function 19H – default drive number returned in AL register.

Function 1AH – set address for disk transfer in DS:DX. If this function is not used, the address CS:0080H will be used.

Function 1BH – Disk FAT (partial) information. After use, DS:BX gives address of start of FAT of default drive in memory, DX contains number of allocation units, AL sectors per byte, CX bytes per sector. Applicable mainly to V.1.x.

Function 1CH – Disk FAT as 1BH, but for specified drive rather than default drive.

Functions 1DH-20H Reserved for future use. *Unofficially* 1FH gets the drive parameter table for the default drive.

Function 21H – random access read using FCB. DS:DX contains address of open FCB, record read into disk transfer address.

Function 22H – random access write using FCB. DS:DX contains address of open FCB, record written from disk transfer address.

Function 23H – file size using FCB. DS:DX contains address of unopened FCB, whose record size values will be altered if the file is found.

Function 24H – random access record number using FCB. DS:DX contains address of open FCB, whose relative record field number will be altered.

Function 25H – interrupt vector set. DS:DX contains address of first byte in interrupt table, and AL contains interrupt reference number.

Function 26H – create new program segment – V.1.x only.

Function 27H – random access block read using FCB. DS:DX contains address of open FCB, CX contains number of records whose size is specified in the FCB. Records are read into the disk transfer address.

Function 28H – random access block write using FCB. DS:DX contains address of open FCB, CX contains number of records to be written from the disk transfer address.

Function 29H – parse command line tail for FCB. AL contains status byte to determine how separator characters, drive numbers, filenames and extensions are treated. After use, ES:DI contains address for FCB, DS:DI contains address for first character following command line.

Function 2AH – Date returned in CX (year), DH (month number), DL (day number in month), and AL (day number in week).

Function 2BH – set date, using CX, DH and DL as above. On Amstrad and other machines with battery-backed clock, 2BH resets the date on this clock.

Function 2CH – time returned in CH (hours), CL (minutes), DH (seconds) and DL (hundredths of seconds).

Function 2DH – set time, using CH, CL, DH, DL as above. Battery-backed clocks will be reset.

Function 2EH – disk file verification set/reset. AL contains 00H to turn verify off, 01H to turn verify on.

The following functions are not used in V.1.x of MS-DOS

Function 2FH – find disk transfer address, place in ES:BX.

Function 30H – find DOS version number, place into AL with figure after decimal point in AH. AL contains 00H if a version prior to 2.0 is being used.

Function 31H – terminate program and stay resident (TSR). AL contains exit code, DX stores number of 16-byte blocks that must remain allocated to the resident program.

Function 32H – *unofficially* used to give address of drive parameter table in DS:BX.

Function 33H – Ctrl-break flag. IF AL set to 00H, Ctrl-Break setting is reported only. With AL = 01H, DL = 0 turns Ctrl-Break off, DL = 1 turns Ctrl-Break on so that it will be checked at each call to DOS rather than on input/output only.

Function 34H – *unofficially* returns in ES:BX address of counter which records when DOS has been entered (so as to prevent re-entry).

Function 35H – find interrupt address for INT number in AL. Address is returned in ES:BX.

Function 36H – find free space on disk, drive number in DL. After use, BX contains number of free clusters, DX total number of clusters on drive, CX number of bytes per sector, AX number of sectors per cluster.

Function 37H – *unofficially* find or reset the command line option character, which is usually /.

Function 38H – find or reset country information, V.2.x can find only. For V.3.x onwards, AL is loaded with FFH, BX contains country number and DS:DX holds address for a buffer which will contain the data (34 bytes max.).

Function 39H – create subdirectory. DS:DX contains address for path name of new subdirectory, using 0H terminator.

Function 3AH – remove subdirectory. DS:DX contains address for path name of subdirectory, terminated with 0H. Subdirectory must be empty, and must not be in current use.

Function 3BH – change current subdirectory. DS:DX contains address for path name of subdirectory, terminated with 0H.

Functions 3CH to 46H were introduced in V.2.0 as a way of making file actions simpler and faster, replacing the File control Block method that was inherited from CP/M with an improved method called File Handles. These functions should be used in any programs being written for file actions. When a file is created, using function 3CH, or opened using function 3DH, a 16-bit number called the *file handle* is placed in the AX register, and this number is from then on used as a reference to the file. In V2.0 onwards, it becomes possible to write to or read from peripherals by using names such as PRN, CON, AUX1 etc. This is made possible by assigning reserved file handle number to these peripherals as follows:

Keyboard input	00H
Screen output	01H
Error report	02H
Auxiliary	03H
Printer	04H

Function 3CH – file create using handle. DS:DX

contains address for string containing drive, path and filename, terminated with 0H. Attribute code is placed in CX. After use, AX contains file handle if carry flag is reset, otherwise AX carries error code.

Function 3DH – file open using handle. DS:DX contains address for string containing drive, path and filename, terminated with 0H. AL contains access code for read and write by owner or other network users. Use only codes 0H (write), 01H (read) or 02H (read and write) if the machine is not to be networked. After use, AX contains file handle or (if carry flag set) an error code.

Function 3EH – file close using handle. BX is used to hold file handle number

Function 3FH – read file or device using handle. BX is used to hold file handle number, CX the number of bytes to read, and DS:DX contains the address for a buffer in memory. After use, AX contains the number of bytes read or (if carry flag set) an error number.

Function 40H – write to file or device using handle. The file handle is placed in BX, the number of bytes to be written in CX, and the buffer address in DS:DX. After use AX contains the number of bytes written or (if carry flag set) an error code.

Function 41H – delete directory entry. The DS:DX registers are used to contain the address of a string containing drive, path and filename, terminated with 0H.

Function 42H – file pointer move. When a file is created or opened, the first byte is available for reading or writing, and the byte position is held as a pointer number. By using this function, the 'pointer' can be moved so as to read any byte out of order. The pointer number is held in CX:DC, the file handle in BX and AL is used to hold a code that determines whether the pointer number is added to the start of the file number, end of the file number or current pointer number. After use, DX:AX stores new pointer number, but if carry flag is set, then AX contains an error code.

Function 43H – File attribute change. DS:DX contains address for a filename string containing drive, path and name, terminated with 0H. AL is set to 00H to report attributes, 01H to alter attributes. CX is used to hold the new set of attribute bits if these are to be changed.

Function 44H – input/output control. File handle

is put into BX, using numbers 00H to 04H (see list above) for devices. Sixteen different forms of the function can be called by using values 00H to 0FH in AL. These are listed in outline here, with no details about register contents.

AL Value	Action
00H	get device channel 16-bit data in DX.
01H	set device channel 16-bit data in DX.
02H	read string from device.
03H	write string to a device.
04H	read string from disk.
05H	write string to disk.
06H	get file or device input status.
07H	get file or device output status.
08H	check for fixed disk.
09H	test is drive local or remote on network.
0AH	test file handle for local or remote.
0BH	change retry count for file sharing in network.
0CH	change device code page.
0DH	multi-action function in V3.2 onwards – used to get parameters, set parameters, format, read track or write track on disk.
0EH	get last logical drive letter.
0FH	assign logical device letter.

Function 45H – file handle duplication. BX contains a file handle, and after the action, AX contains a handle number for the same file.

Function 46H – file handle forced duplication. BX contains one file handle and CX another. After use, both handles refer to the same file, and if the CX handle referred to another open file, that file is closed.

Function 47H – get current directory. DS:SI contains address of a memory buffer, DL contains a drive number. After use, the buffer contains the string with directory path (no drive letter) terminated with 00H.

Function 48H – memory allocation. BX is used to specify number of 16-byte units (paragraphs) to be allocated. After use, AX contains segment address.

Function 49H – memory release. ES contains segment address of memory block which is to be returned for re-use.

Function 4AH – memory re-allocation. ES contains segment address of allocated block, BX contains number of 16-byte paragraphs in modified block.

Function 4BH – child load and execute. Allows a program that is running (the *parent*) to load and run another program (the *child*). Memory must have been de-allocated using function 4BH, because MS-DOS normally assigns the whole of available memory to a program. Used by applications programs to allow use of MS-DOS commands by making COMMAND.COM a child program. AL contains code determining if child is to be loaded and run, or overlaid at a specified address and not run. DS:DX contains address for string of drive, path and filename for child program, terminated with 00H. EX:BX contains address of memory that contains any information needed by the child program (the environment parameters)

Function 4CH – terminates a program. Returns a code in AL which can be picked up as an ERRORLEVEL code in a batch file (or for a child program with Function 4DH).

Function 4DH – get child program return code. The AL register contains the return codes:

Normal termination	00H
Ctrl-Break used	01H
Error caused termination	02H
TSR	03H

Function 4EH – search for matching filename. DS:DX contains address of string containing drive, path and filename (wildcards permitted), using 00H as terminator. CX can contain attribute bits. If a matching file is found in the directory, file details will be loaded into the disk transfer area.

Function 4FH – find next matching file. Continues action that was set up by use of Function 4EH.

Function 50H – *unofficially* designates a program to be current if its ID number is loaded into BX before calling 50H.

Function 51H – *unofficially* gets the ID number for a current program in BX register.

Function 52H – *unofficially* gets address in ES:BX for a table of values held in memory.

Function 53H – *unofficially* gets into DS:SI address for a BIOS parameter block, with ES:BP containing address for drive parameter table.

Function 54H – verify state. After use, AL = 00H if verify is off, AL = 01H if verify is on.

Function 55H – reserved for later use.

Function 56H – file rename. DS:DX is used to hold the address of the string that contains drive, path and filename, ending with 00H, and ES:DI contains the new string (using the *same* drive).

Function 57H – read/write time and date on file. BX must contain the file handle. If AL = 00H, then after use file date is in DX, time in CX. If AL = 01H, then the values in DX and CX will be written to the file.

Function 58H – memory allocation method. When memory is to be allocated, MS-DOS can allocate by searching either from the start of memory or from the end, and by allocating any block that is large enough, or looking for the block that is closest to the required size. AL is used to hold the get (00H0 or set (01H) code, and AX is used to return the current strategy code, or BX to contain the code that is to be used.

Function 59H – extended error messages. Must be used immediately following an error with BX set to 00H. After use the error code is in AX, with an error class code in BH, advised action in BL and error source (unknown, block device, network, serial device or memory) code in CH.

Function 5AH – create temporary (scratchpad) file. DS:DX contains address for string containing path, ending with backslash and zero. After use, DS:DX will contain specifier string for the temporary file, ending with 00H.

Function 5BH – create new file (compare 3CH). DS:DX contains address for specifier string, CX contains attribute code bits. After use, AX contains file handle, *but* not if the file already exists.

Function 5CH – file lock/unlock for networking. File handle is placed in BX, and AL holds 00H if file is to be locked (01H to unlock). Registers CX:DX contain the address for the start of the region to lock, with SI:DI holding the length of the region.

Function 5DH – *unofficially* used to obtain information on some types of errors

Function 5EH – used for networking with 5EH in AH and codes 00H – 03H in AL.

AL = 00H	get machine name.
AL = 02H	send set-up string to printer.
AL = 03H	show set-up string for printer.

Function 5F – used for networking with 5F in AH and codes 02H-04 in AL.

AL = 02H	get list linking device name with network name.
AL = 03H	alter redirection of device to network name.
AL = 04H	cancel redirection.

Functions 60H and 61H not currently used.

Function 62H – find PSP. The Program Segment Prefix is the table in memory which occupies bytes 0000H to 00FFH (so that the program starts at 0100H in the segment). This table contains data about the program such as terminate address, exit address for Ctrl-Break and so on. Use 62H in AH to call, and after use BX has segment address of the PSP.

Function 63H – used in V2.25 only, do not make use of this function

Function 64H – not currently used.

Function 65H – get code page.

Function 66H – set code page.

Function 67H – set number of permitted file handles. The default is 20, and to change this number, call the function with BX containing the new number of handles. On V.3.x, avoid using even numbers or numbers close to FFFFH.

Function 68H – clear buffers. BX contains a file handle and when the function is used, all buffers associated with the file are cleared and the directory is updated.

Error codes

When an error occurs during an MS-DOS function, the carry flag will be set, because the state of this flag is the easiest to test. When this happens, an error code will be returned, usually in AX, and many of the codes are standardised, though some functions return error codes of their own. The standard error codes are shown below, with codes 01H to 12H being used on all versions of MS-DS, codes 20H onwards on versions 3.0 onwards.

Code	Meaning
01H	function number not valid
02H	file not found

03H	path not found
04H	no spare handles (too many open files)
05H	access denied
06H	handle not valid
07H	control block in memory corrupted
08H	out of memory
09H	memory block address not valid
0AH	environment not valid
0BH	format not valid
0CH	access code not valid
0DH	data not valid
0EH	reserved
0FH	drive specification not valid
10H	cannot delete current subdirectory
11H	not same device
12H	no more files

The following error codes apply to network use and will not be found when a single-user machine is involved.

20H	sharing violation
21H	lock violation
22H	disk change not valid
23H	FCB not available
24H	sharing buffer overflow
25H - 31H	reserved
32H	network request denied
33H	remote computer not receiving
34H	name duplicated on network
35H	network name not found
36H	network busy
37H	device does not exist on network
38H	BIOS command limit on network exceeded
39H	hardware error on network adapter
3AH	network response incorrect
3BH	network error (unknown)
3CH	remote adapter incompatible
3DH	print queue full
3EH	print queue not full
3FH	print file deleted
40H	network name deleted
41H	access denied
42H	device type incorrect

43H	network name not found
44H	network name limit exceeded
45H	exceeded network BIOS session limit
46H	temporary pause
47H	network request denied
48H	redirection temporarily halted
49H - 4FH	reserved
50H	file already exists
51H	reserved
52H	cannot create directory entry
53H	INT 24 failure
54H	too many redirections
55H	duplicate redirection
56H	password not valid
57H	parameter not valid
58H	fault in network device

High-level languages

In theory, a high level language should make it unnecessary to use MS-DOS routines directly, but the ability to call assembly language modules and to insert MS-DOS calls into a high level language is most useful, since it can often make a considerable difference to program execution times. For this reason, practically all high-level languages have some provision for interfacing with MS-DOS, and this applies even to C, which is often regarded as being very close to assembly language.

Easy access to machine-code modules and to MS-DOS calls is particularly useful for languages like PASCAL which are often deficient in statements that allow for system programming as distinct from applications programming. Turbo-PASCAL (from Borland International) is probably the best-known of all PASCAL dialects, and it provides for MS-DOS calls with the function **MsDos()**. This takes as its argument in the brackets a record variable which consists of ten integers, the contents of the ten registers. In this way, quantities can be assigned to the registers and the MS-DOS INT 21 carried out from within Turbo-PASCAL.

Borland's Turbo BASIC also offers many facilities for interacting with MS-DOS and machine code. The $INLINE statement can be used to enter hex bytes into a code module that can be called by a label name. The $SEGMENT statement allows a new code segment to be chosen. The main facilities, however, make use of CALL. This can be to an INLINE piece of assembly language, as an ABSOLUTE call to a stated address in memory, or as an INTERRUPT call to MS-DOS. When **CALL INTERRUPT &H21** is used to make an MS-DOS call, the registers can be loaded by using the REG statement, using a reference number for each register (0 for flags up to 9 for ES) and the number that is to be loaded into the register.

Zortech **C** provides for inline assembly and the calling of machine-code or assembly-language modules. There is also a library set of functions that allow both DOS calls and direct calls to the BIOS, mainly for file actions, and the INTDOS function which allows the INT 21 to be used after setting up a structure to contain register contents.

Disk and file organization

One of the problems that has been due to the evolution of computers over the years is the proliferation of disk standards. If the very early disk formats are ignored, the current set of floppy disk standards includes:

5.25″ disks of 360K capacity (DSDD 40 track 9 sector)

5.25″ disks of 1.2Mb capacity (DS 80 track 15 sector)

3.5″ disks of 720K capacity (DS 80 track 9 sector)

3.5″ disks of 1.44Mb capacity (DS 80 track 18 sector)

and MS-DOS has to cope also with hard disks which can use a number of *platters* (any number from 2 upwards), with each platter using 306 tracks on each side.

When FORMAT is used, the tracks and sectors are marked out, and data is written to selected tracks and sectors. This data consists of the boot record, the file allocation table (FAT) and the file directory, and all three can be examined and altered using DEBUG. Careless alteration in any of these groups can make a disk unreadable other than by another user of DEBUG.

The boot record consists of instructions for loading and running the SYS (hidden) files that comprise the MS-DOS system. If these have already been loaded, this part of the disk will not be used, and on a disk formatted as a data disk the SYS files would not be present in any case. Attempting to use this disk at startup will cause an error message because the system files have not been located. The boot record also contains the data about the structure of the disk, filling most of the sector.

Example
DEBUG
-L 0 0 0 1
-D 0000
-D

gives the dump shown in Figure 8.1 in edited form: in which the first three bytes of EB 34 90 are a jump instruction to find the system tracks if this disk is in the drive when the machine is started. The disk has been formatted using MS-DOS 3.2, so that this information is put in following the jump command. The remainder of this first sector is used for the program which will load in the SYS files, and is not connected with the files on the disk.

The FAT exists as two copies, only one of which is used by MS-DOS. The thinking here is that if the FAT that is used by MS-DOS is damaged in some way, then it might be possible to copy over the second one to replace it, but if the disk has been mechanically damaged this is not useful. It does, however, allow you to make a copy with DISKCOPY and copy the second FAT into the position of the first FAT on that disk, so making the allocation table readable. The FAT, as its name suggests, shows how a file is placed on the disk in terms of clusters. For a DSDD 5.25″ disk, a cluster is 2 sectors, for higher density disks it is one sector, and for hard disks it will be a larger number of sectors, depending on the size of the disk. The FAT is used by the directory to find where the pieces of a file are placed on the disk so that the file can be read.

Using DEBUG again, the start of a FAT from one of my disks looks (after editing) like Figure 8.2.

In this example, the FAT is short because only two files exist on the sample disk. Because the FAT deals in 12-bit numbers, the hex bytes shown in the dump should be gathered in threes, which makes the start of the FAT look like:

FDF FFF 034 000 560 000 780 000 9A0 000

The first two 12-bit units will always be the same for a disk formatted with this version of MS-DOS,

```
0000  EB 34 90 4D 53 44 4F 53-33 2E 32 00 02 02 01 00   .4.MSDOS3.2.....
0010  02 70 00 D0 02 FD 02 00-09 00 00 02 00 00 00 00   .p..............
0020  00 00 00 00 00 00 00 00-00 00 00 00 00 00 00 0F   ................
0030  00 00 00 00 01 00 FA 33-C0 8E D0 BC 00 7C 16 07   .......3.....|..
0040  BB 78 00 36 C5 37 1E 56-16 53 BF 2B 7C B9 0B 00   .x.6.7.V.S.+!...
0050  FC AC 26 80 3D 00 74 03-26 8A 05 AA 8A C4 E2 F1   ..&.=.t.&.......
0060  06 1F 89 47 02 C7 07 2B-7C FB 16 FD 7D CD 13      ...G...+!...}..
0070  72 66 A0 10 7C 98 F7 26-16 7C 03 06 1C 7C 03 06   rf..!...&.!...
0080  0E 7C A3 3F 7C A3 37 F7-26 16 7C B8 20 00 F7 37   .!.?!.7!...&...
0090  1E 0B 7C 03 C3 48 F7 F3-01 06 37 7C BB 00 05 A1   ..!..H....7!...
00A0  3F 7C E8 94 00 B0 01 E8-A9 00 72 19 8B FB B9 0B   ?!........r....
00B0  00 BE C5 7D F3 A6 75 0D-8D 7F 20 BE D0 7D B9 0B   ...}..u... ..}..
00C0  00 F3 A6 74 18 BE 76 7D-E8 61 00 32 E4 CD 16 5E   ...t..v}.a.2...^
00D0  1F 8F 04 8F 44 02 CD 19-BE AF 7D EB EB A1 1C 05   ....D.....}....
00E0  33 D2 F7 36 0B 7C FE C0-A2 3C 7C A1 37 7C A3 3D   3..6.!...<!.7.=
00F0  7C BB 00 07 A1 37 7C E8-3F 00 A1 18 7C 2A 06 3B   !...7!.?...!.*.;
```

Figure 8.1

```
0000  FD FF FF 03 40 00 05 60-00 07 80 00 09 A0 00 0B   ....@..'........
0010  C0 00 0D E0 00 0F 00 01-11 20 01 13 40 01 15 60   ......... ..@..'
0020  01 17 80 01 19 A0 01 1B-C0 01 1D E0 01 1F 00 02   ................
0030  21 20 02 23 40 02 25 60-02 27 80 02 29 A0 02 2B   ! .#@.%'.'..).+
0040  C0 02 2D E0 02 2F 00 03-31 20 03 33 40 03 35 60   ..-../..1 .3@.5'
0050  03 37 80 03 39 A0 03 3B-C0 03 3D E0 03 3F 00 04   .7..9..;..=..?..
0060  41 20 04 43 40 04 45 60-04 47 80 04 AF FF 04 4B   A .C@.E'.G.....K
0070  F0 FF 00 00 00 00 00 00-00 00 00 00 00 00 00 00   ................
```

Figure 8.2

and the real FAT information starts with unit 3, which will indicate the number for the current cluster and the next cluster, because of the peculiar way in which the bits are coded, the set **034 000** is used to mean clusters 3 and 4, with **560 000** meaning clusters 5 and 6, as illustrated here –

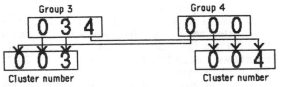

Figure 8.3   12-bit data to cluster number conversion

Even allowing for the oddities of the coding system, however, the numbers show that this is not a fragmented disk. In general, you will not need to work on the FAT directly, and if you intend to do so you will need detailed information on the way that the cluster number is converted into 12-bit form and used. The directory entry for a file gives the starting cluster for that file, with the first file on a disk always starting at cluster 2 (the clusters are numbered from 1, with the boot record, FAT and Directory counting as clusters 0 and 1). If you *do* need to work on the FAT entries, you are strongly recommended to use a program which will work out the logic of the entries for you, because working on the FAT numbers by hand will at the mildest cause eye-strain and at worst brain-strain.

The directory entry is considerably more accessible and is more likely to be needed. The entry for each file consists of 32 bytes, of which the first 11 are used for the filename and its extension, using spaces (20H) to pad the name out if it is not of the full 11 characters. The first byte is significant:

00	has not been used
2E	a directory entry
E5	a deleted file

The 12th byte (byte 0BH, counting from byte 00H) is the attribute byte, and the next ten bytes are reserved for future use. The following two bytes, numbers 16H and 17H are used for time, and bytes 18H, 19H for date. The most important bytes are 1AH and 1BH, which give the number of the first cluster for the file. As usual, the low order byte is stored first, so that 2F 01 means cluster 012FH. The first file always starts at cluster 02H. The last four bytes in the directory entry give the size of the file in bytes, in low-to-high byte order.

Example DEBUG has been used to read the directory of a disk which contains only two files in its visible directory. Figure 8.4 shows the (edited) result.

At some time, the whole of this disk has had its files deleted, and two new files have been recorded on top. For the first file, the entry shows the name, padded with spaces (20H), and the extension of TXT. The attribute byte is 20H, meaning that the archive bit is set. The time entry is 1C82, and to interpret this it has to be reversed in order as 821C and then written in bit bunches of 5-6-5 as:

Binary	10000	010000	11100
Denary	16	16	28

– in which the units are hours, minutes and then pairs of seconds, so that the last figure should be multiplied by 2 to get 56, for a time of 16:16:56. The date bytes are treated similarly, so that the entry 5412 is written as *1254* and converted as:

Binary	0001001	0010	10100
Denary	9	2	20

– in which the units are years (since 1980, the zero year PC), then month number, then day number, so that the file was created on 20th February, 1989.

The next two sectors are 02 00, giving the number 0002 for the starting cluster, and finally the length number is given as 80 19 01 00, sp that the length of the file in bytes is 00011980H, which is 72064 bytes, the number which the DIR command will print. The listing also shows a similar set of entries for the next file, called PDSPRF.TXT, but the remaining entries to the directory all start with the E5H byte, meaning that they are deleted entries. File recovery programs will place a letter into the first byte of the name, and then re-build the FAT starting at the first cluster number that is carried in the directory.

The PSP

When a program is loaded into the computer, the first 100H (255) bytes of the memory that contains the file are used to hold data about the program, the

```
0000  50 44 53 35 20 20 20 20 20-54 58 54 20 00 00 00 00  PDS5    TXT ....
0010  00 00 00 00 1C 20 20 82-54 12 02 00 80 19 01 00  ........T.....
0020  50 44 53 50 52 46 20 20 20-54 58 54 20 00 00 00 00  PDSPRF   TXT ...
0030  00 00 00 00 B2 7C-50 12 49 00 00 0A 00 00  .......!P.I...
0040  E5 45 43 4F 20 20 20 20-46 4E 54 20 00 00 00 00  .ECO    FNT ..
0050  00 00 00 00 79 82-BD 0E CF 00 76 5C 00 00  ....y...v\..
0060  E5 41 49 4E 20 20 20 20-46 4E 54 20 00 00 00 00  .AIN    FNT ..
0070  00 00 00 00 B3 82-BD 0E E7 00 F6 59 00 00  ....y...
0080  E5 49 4D 50 4C 45 58 20-46 4E 54 20 00 00 00 00  .IMPLEX FNT ..
0090  00 00 00 00 CD 82-BD 0E FE 00 2C 47 00 00  ....,.G..
00A0  E5 47 41 20 20 20 20 20-56 47 44 20 00 00 00 00  .GA     VGD ..
```

Figure 8.4

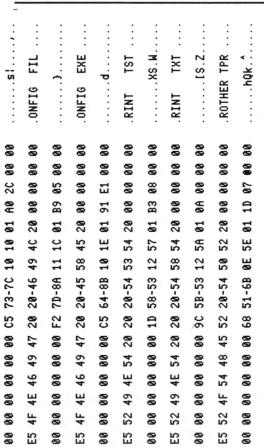

Figure 8.4 *contd*

```
0160  E5 41 4E 4F 4E 20 20 20 20-54 50 52 20 00 00 00 00   .ANON    TPR ....
0170  00 00 00 00 00 61 51-C3 0E 60 01 FB 00 00 00        .....aQ.'.....
0180  E5 45 4E 54 52 4F 4E 20-54 50 52 20 00 00 00        .ENTRON TPR ....
0190  00 00 00 00 68 51-6B 0E 61 01 20 01 00 00           ....hQk.a. ...
01A0  E5 49 54 4F 48 20 20 20-54 50 52 20 00 00 00        .ITOH   TPR ....
01B0  00 00 00 00 68 51-51 0F 62 01 00 07 00 00           ....hQQ.b.....
01C0  E5 41 54 41 50 52 4F 44-54 50 52 20 00 00 00        .ATAPRODTPR ....
01D0  00 00 00 00 D5 7C-7F 10 00 00 00 00 00 00           .......|......
01E0  E5 41 54 53 4F 55 54 48-54 50 52 20 00 00 00        .ATSOUTHTPR ....
01F0  00 00 00 00 68 51-6B 0E 00 00 00 00 00 00           ....hQk......
```

Figure 8.4 *contd*

Program Segment Prefix or PSP. This is why DEBUG always start at relative address 0100, the start of the program, rather than relative address 0000. The function of the PSP is to allow MS-DOS to work more easily with the program, locating important addresses, such as the address to go to after program termination, or after Ctrl-Break has been used. It is most unlikely that you will ever need to use DEBUG to modify a PSP, so that there is little point in noting the functions of the various bytes.

Appendix A – Hex notation

Hexadecimal means scale of sixteen, and the reason that it is used so extensively is that it is naturally suited to representing binary bytes. Four bits, half of a byte, will represent numbers which lie in the range 0 to 15 in the ordinary (denary, or scale of ten) number scale. This is the range of one hex digit. Since we don't have symbols for digits higher than 9, we have to use the letters A,B,C,D,E, and F to supplement the digits 0 to 9 in the hex scale.

Denary	Hex	Binary
00	00	0000
01	01	0001
02	02	0010
03	03	0011
04	04	0100
05	05	0101
06	06	0110
07	07	0111
08	08	1000
09	09	1001
10	0A	1010
11	0B	1011
12	0C	1100
13	0D	1101
14	0E	1110
15	0F	1111

The advantage is that a byte can be represented by a two-digit number, and a complete 16-bit word or address by a four-digit number. Converting between binary and hex is much simpler than converting between binary and denary. The leading zero in a number like **0B** doesn't have to be written, but programmers get into the habit of writing a data byte with two digits and an address with four even if fewer digits are needed. The number that follows 0F is 10, sixteen in denary, and the scale then repeats to 1F, thirty-one, which is followed by 20. The maximum size of a single byte, 255 in denary, is FF in hex.

When we write hex numbers, it's usual to mark them in some way so that you don't confuse them with denary numbers. There's not much chance of confusing a number like 3E with a denary number, but a number like 26 might be hex or denary. The convention that is followed by many programmers is to use a capital H to mark a hex number, with the

H-sign placed after the number. For example, the number 47H means hex 47, but plain 47 would mean denary forty-seven. Another method is to use the hashmark before the number, so that #47 would mean the same as 47H. When you write hex numbers for an MS-DOS program on paper, it's a good idea to follow one of these conventions. When you are actually typing hex numbers into the computer, for example when you are using DEBUG, you don't need to add the 'H' or the '#'. Many of the MS-DOS machine-code utilities assume that you will type in hex numbers, and they will not work with anything else. You might think that this could be awkward, but it's not, because DEBUG provides you with some useful assistance, like a hex arithmetic calculator. The only awkwardness is to remember when you must use the letter H following a hex number, but we'll come to that later.

Now the great value of hex code is how closely it corresponds to binary code. If you look at the hex-binary table above, you can see that #9 is 1001 in binary and #F is 1111. The hex number #9F is therefore just 10011111 in binary – you simply write down the binary digits that correspond to the hex digits. Taking another example, the hex byte #B8 is 10111000, because #B is 1011 and #8 is 1000. The conversion in the opposite direction is just as easy-you group the binary digits in fours, starting at the least significant (right-hand) side of the number, and then convert each group into its corresponding hex digit.

Example
Convert 2CH to binary:
2H is 0010 binary
CH is 1100 binary
so that 2CH is 00101100 binary

Example
Convert 4A7FH to binary
4H is 0100 binary
AH is 1010 binary
7H is 0111 binary
FH is 1111 binary
so that 4A7FH is 0100101001111111 binary

Example
Convert 3000:41E6 to binary

This is the two-part form of the address 341E6,

which is converted as above to the 20-bit binary form:

`00110100000111100110`

Example
Convert `01101011` to hex
the group `1011` is BH
the group `0110` is 6H
so that `01101011` is 6BH

Example
Convert `11000101101101101110` to hex
group in fours starting at the right hand side:
`1110` is EH
`0110` is 6H
`1011` is BH
`0101` is 5H
`1100` is CH
so that the complete number is C5B6EH. This could be coded in two-part for as:
`C000:5B6E`

Negative numbers

Negative numbers are not used to a large extent in assembly language work because addresses are usually shown in absolute form, either with the full CS:IP value or specifying an IP value for the current segment. One notable exception, however, is the short jump to a label name in an assembly language program, perhaps jumping to a step which is 30 steps ahead of its present address. This sort of thing can be programmed by using a JMP command which is followed by the word **short** and then a label name for the point to which you want to jump. The **jmp** code for this type of instruction is EBH, and using one single byte following this code allows a jump of up to 127 steps forward or 128 steps back, measured from the address of the following instruction.

If you want to jump back to a previous step, then, you will need to use a negative number for this data byte. This is very common, because it's one way that a loop can be programmed in machine code. It also has the advantage that shifting the program about in the memory requires no adjustment to be made to these jumps because they involve no fixed address values. For this type of jump, then, you need to know how a negative number appears in hex. When you write code in assembler language there is no need to know how the code will appear, but when you look at the written code using DEBUG, it is often useful to be able to check that these jump bytes are of the correct value. In addition, if you use the H command of DEBUG, followed by two numbers, you'll get the sum of the numbers, and their difference, printed. As often as not, one of these numbers will be negative – but will you know?

What makes it awkward is that there is no negative sign in hex arithmetic. There isn't one in binary either. The conversion of a number to its negative form is done by a method called complementing, illustrated here:

Binary number	00110110 (denary 36)
inverted	11001001
add 1	11001010 (denary −36)

– this involves complementing the number (interchanging 0 and 1) and then adding 1 to the result. To find the 8-bit equivalent for −5, for example:

number +5 is	00000101
invert	11111010
add 1	11111011
	which is −5 in 8-bit binary.

At first sight, and very often at second, third, and fourth, it looks entirely crazy. When you are dealing with a single byte number, for example, the denary form of the number −1 is 255. You are using a large positive number to represent a small negative one, and it begins to make more sense when you look at the numbers written in binary. The eight-bit numbers that can be regarded as negative all start with a 1 and the positive numbers all start with a 0. The microprocessor can find out which is which just by testing the left-hand bit, the most significant bit.

It's a simple method, which the machine can use efficiently, but it does have disadvantages for mere humans. One of these disadvantages is that the digits of a negative number are not the same as those of a positive number. For example, in denary −40 uses the same digits as +40, In hex, −40 becomes D8H and +40 becomes 28H. The denary number −85 becomes ABH and +85 becomes 55H. It's not at all obvious that one is the negative form of the other. The second disadvantage is that humans cannot distinguish between a single byte number which is intended to be negative and one which is just a byte greater than 127. For example, does 9FH mean 159 or does it mean – 97? The short answer is that the human operator doesn't have to worry. The microprocessor will use the number correctly no matter how we happen to think of it. The snag is that we have to know what this correct use is in each case. Throughout books that deal with machine code programming, you will see the words 'signed' and 'unsigned' used. A signed number is one that may be negative or positive. For a single byte number, values of 0 to 7FH are positive, and values of 80H to FFH are negative. This corresponds to denary numbers 0 to 127 for positive values and 128 to 255 for negative. Unsigned numbers are always taken as positive. If you find the number 9CH described as signed, then, you know it's treated as a negative number (it's more than 80H). If it's described as unsigned, then it's positive, and its value is obtained simply by converting. The snag here is that when we make use of the H command of DEBUG, it will not deal with signs in single bytes. If, for example, you type: H 2A 2B then what you will see underneath is 0055, the sum, and FFFF, which is the difference. You get FFFF rather than FF, because the H command works with hex numbers of four digits. It's not a real problem, because all you have to do is to ignore the first two digits when you are working with single bytes. There's nothing in DEBUG, however, that will convert a denary number into a hex number for you.

Appendix B – The 8088/8086 CPU

The use of MS-DOS cannot be separated from the use of the microprocessor chip, and throughout Chapters 7 and 8 of this book, these registers have been referred to without explanation.

Each register is a 16-bit store which is located inside the microprocessor chip rather than as part of the main memory. Because the registers are internal to the microprocessor, an instruction that affects the contents of a register can be carried out very much more quickly than an instruction that affects the contents of any memory location. The registers of the 8088/8086 microprocessor types can be grouped into general-purpose, pointer/index, segment and flags. The segment registers are used, as the name suggests, mainly to store segment numbers for the different parts of an EXE program – for a COM program, these registers would normally be set up so that they all contained the same segment address. All addresses that are used to refer to memory will make use of the numbers in the segment registers, so that addresses in EXE programs will be of two types, the short type which use an address that is in the 64K of the current segment, or the long type which will require the address in the segment register to be changed. The segment registers are the code segment **CS**, the data segment **DS**, the stack segment SS, and the extra segment **ES**.

The CS register is used, as the name suggests, to maintain the segment address for program bytes (the IP register is used for locating each byte in the segment). The actual address of a byte in memory is formed by adding a hex zero to the CS number and adding the number stored in the IP register; this is written as CS:IP. Programs of the COM type will use one single segment for all purposes, and small EXE programs will use only one code segment number, so that each memory reference is a short one, within the segment. The DS register is used to hold a segment number that will be used for data within the program, which could include a buffer space. The ES register is often used for the same purposes if there is a large-scale need for data to be stored. Assemblers generally will assume that when an instruction requires data then the DS register will locate the correct segment, and another register will provide the offset number (the number of bytes into the segment). The 8086 microprocessor can deal with data more rapidly if all data is aligned on an even-numbered address (the start of a 16-bit number).

The SS register locates the segment that is used for the stack, the first-in-first-out form of memory for temporarily storing quantities such as register contents during an interrupt or a subroutine call. It is unusual to need as much memory as a whole segment can provide for a stack, because many programs can run without difficulties on a stack of 256 bytes or less. The top end of another segment can often be used for the stack, so that the SS value may be the same as the DS or even the CS value. The program itself has to declare how the segment registers will be used, and must **also** ensure that correct initial values are placed into these registers. Different assemblers have slightly different methods of dealing with these requirements.

The general purpose registers are used for manipulating data, using arithmetic and logic commands. There are four 16-bit registers of this type, and each of them can be used as two separate 8-bit registers. The register that comes in for the heaviest use is the accumulator, and assemblers use **AX** to mean the complete 16-bit accumulator register, with **AL** meaning the lower 8 bits and **AH** meaning the upper 8 bits. The other general-purpose registers are **BX** (which can be divided as **BH** and **BL**), **CX** (which can be divided as **CH** and **CL**) and **DX** (which can be divided as **DH** and **DL**). The BX register is referred to as the Base register, and is often used as an address store in commands that make use of tables in memory. The **CX** register is called the Count register, referring to its use in holding numbers that can be incremented or decremented during a count. The **DX** register is the Data register, often used as an alternative to **AX**.

All of these registers can be used for manipulating data, but some instruction will assume the specialised use of a register. For example, the **jcxz** assembler command will cause a jump to a new address if the content of register **CX** is zero. Many of the looping commands apply to the contents of **CX** also, including the **loop** itself (decrements CX and branches to a new address if CX does not contain zero). Similarly, the table lookup command **xlat** makes use of an address in the BX register. The index registers are used to indicate positions in memory, and of these the stack pointer **SP** is maintained automatically by the microprocessor to show the address of the next vacant position in the stack. The base pointer **BP** is used, often along with BX, in table indexing, and the source index (**SI**) and destination index (**DI**) registers are used in moving blocks of bytes from one set of memory locations to another. The registers other than the stack pointer can also be used for other addressing purposes. the **SI** and **DI** registers are used by several block move instructions such as **lods, stos, movs, cmps,** and **scas**. The direction flag in the flag registers is 0 when index registers are incrementing, 1 when they are decrementing.

The remaining registers are the instruction pointer **IP** and the flag registers. The IP register carries the relative address (the address inside the segment) of the current instruction that the microprocessor is executing, and in the course of a program will be automatically incremented in order to move from one instruction to the next. There is no provision for altering the content of the IP register directly. The flag register is a collection of separate bits each of which indicates the result of the previous action, as noted in Chapter 7 dealing with DEBUG. Some flags can be set or reset individually, but there is no direct way of transferring the whole contents of the flag register. If the flag register has to be altered it can be done by way of the stack by pushing the contents of another register on to the stack and popping this (using **popf**) to the flag register. The contents of the flag register can similarly be transferred to another 16-bit register.

Appendix C – ASCII codes in Denary and Hex

No.	Hex	Char
32	20	(space)
33	21	!
34	22	"
35	23	£
36	24	$
37	25	%
38	26	&
39	27	'
40	28	(
41	29	)
42	2A	*
43	2B	+
44	2C	,
45	2D	-
46	2E	.
47	2F	/
48	30	0
49	31	1
50	32	2
51	33	3
52	34	4
53	35	5
54	36	6
55	37	7
56	38	8
57	39	9
58	3A	:
59	3B	;
60	3C	<
61	3D	=
62	3E	>
63	3F	?
64	40	@
65	41	A
66	42	B
67	43	C
68	44	D
69	45	E
70	46	F
71	47	G
72	48	H
73	49	I
74	4A	J

75	4B	K
76	4C	L
77	4D	M
78	4E	N
79	4F	O
80	50	P
81	51	Q
82	52	R
83	53	S
84	54	T
85	55	U
86	56	V
87	57	W
88	58	X
89	59	Y
90	5A	Z
91	5B	[
92	5C	\
93	5D	]
94	5E	^
95	5F	_
96	60	`
97	61	a
98	62	b
99	63	c
100	64	d
101	65	e
102	66	f
103	67	g
104	68	h
105	69	i
106	6A	j
107	6B	k
108	6C	l
109	6D	m
110	6E	n
111	6F	o
112	70	p
113	71	q
114	72	r
115	73	s
116	74	t
117	75	u
118	76	v
119	77	w
120	78	x
121	79	y
122	7A	z

123	7B	{
124	7C	¦
125	7D	}
126	7E	∿
127	7F	

Appendix D – Some useful public domain and shareware utilities

These programs are all available from:

The Public Domain Software Library,
Winscombe House,
Beacon Road,
Crowborough,
Sussex TN6 1UL

– the catalogue numbers shown in the list are those of PDSL, to whom I am grateful for permission to print these extracts.

0534 A86 Assembler for 8086/8088/80286 code. This is an excellent assembler package which is fully capable of working on large files.

0825ABC File Conversion Utilities. A set of three disks which allow various word-processor, spreadsheet and database files to be converted to other formats.

0870AB Unprotect Utilities. Allow copy protection to be removed on the few programs that still use such systems, so that backups can be made and programs restored to hard disks if they have been removed.

0787AB Hard disk utilities. Programs to check the state of a hard disk, reorganize files, unerase, lock out bad sectors etc.

0869 Backfast. A utility for hard-disk backup and retrieval of selected files, using floppy disks.

0344 Three Text Editors. Three useful editors for creating batch and other text files.

1217 Batch file utilities. A set of programs to enhance the use of batch files by adding extra facilities.

1090 Text file filters. A set of utilities for text files, such as line counting, putting in omitted capitals at the start of a sentence, blank line remover, duplicate line remover etc.

U632 Printer utilities including PRTSCFX which allows graphics characters in text screens to be printed on the Epson series of printers.

Index

ORDER FORM

QTY				TOTAL
POCKET BOOKS				
Newnes MS-DOS Pocket Book				
.... 2nd Edition	Sinclair	0 7506 0328 3	£9.95	....
.... Newnes 8086 Family Pocket Book	Sinclair	0 434 91872 5	£10.95	....
.... Newnes Hard Disk Pocket Book	Allen	0 434 90064 8	£12.95	....
.... Newnes MAC User's Pocket Book	Heath	0 7506 0083 7	£12.95	....
.... Newnes PC Printer's Pocket Book	Morris	0 7506 0197 3	£12.95	....
.... Newnes PC User's Pocket Book	Reid	0 7506 0085 3	£12.95	....
Newnes Computer Engineer's				
.... Pocket Book Second edition	Tooley	0 434 91969 1	£10.95	....
Newnes Data Communications				
.... Pocket Book	Tooley	0 434 92007 X	£9.95	....
STEP-BY STEP SERIES				
.... Using dBASE IV	Carter	0 434 90251 9	£14.95	....
.... Using Disk & RAM Utilities	Sinclair	0 434 91892 X	£14.95	....
.... Using Lotus 1-2-3 Macros	Sinclair	0 7506 0198 1	£16.95	....
.... Using Lotus 1-2-3 Release 3	Morris	0 434 91292 1	£14.95	....
.... Using MS Word Version 5	Carter	0 434 90316 7	£14.95	....
.... Using Quick BASIC 4.5	Morris	0 7506 0220 1	£14.95	....
Using Q&A on the				
.... IBM and Compatibles	Carter	0 434 90224 1	£14.95	....
.... Using Superbase 2 & 4	Tennick	0 7506 0042 X	£14.95	....
.... Using Windows 3	Tennick	0 7506 0080 2	£14.95	....
.... Using Word for Windows	Balfe	0 7506 0205 8	£14.95	....
.... Using Wordperfect Version 5.0	Gautier	0 434 90656 5	£14.95	....
.... Using Wordstar 5, 5.5 & 6	Balfe	0 7506 0341 0	£14.95	....
.... Using MS-DOS 3.3 to 4.1	Balfe	0 434 92382 6	£14.95	....
Using MS-DOS on the				
.... Amstrad PC 1512/1640	Sinclair	0 434 91842 3	£9.95	....
.... Exploiting the Amstrad PCW 9512	Campbell	0 7506 0075 6	£14.95	....
.... Using the Amstrad PCW9512	Campbell	0 7506 0169 8	£10.95	....
Using Printers on the				
.... Amstrad PC1512/1640	Gee	0 43490654 9	£14.95	....
Using the Amstrad PC1512/1640				
.... Second Edition	Morris	0 434 91266 2	£12.95	....
.... Using Ability on the Amstrad PC	Kennington	0 434 90221 7	£12.95	....
Using Data Communications				
.... on the Amstrad PC1512/1640	James	0 434 90895 9	£14.95	....
Using Desktop Publishing				
.... on the Amstrad PC	Campbell	0 434 90213 6	£12.95	....
Using Lotus 1-2-3				
.... on the Amstrad PC	Humpage	0 434 90802 9	£12.95	....
Using SuperCalc 3				
.... on the Amstrad PC	McBride	0 434 91221 2	£12.95	....
.... Using dBASEIII on the Amstrad PC	Roberts	0 434 91742 7	£12.95	....
OTHERS				
.... Lotus Symphony 2.0 Handbook	Morris	0 434 91302 2	£16.95	....
Successful Spreadsheets				
.... Using SuperCalc	McBride	0 434 91277 8	£14.95	....

TOTAL CARRIED FORWARD

TOTAL

QTY				TOTAL
.... Using Networking and Communications Software in Business	McBride	0 434 91274 3	£14.95	....
.... Using SuperCalc 5 in Business Spreadsheets in 3 dimensions	McBride	0 434 91308 1	£27.50	....
.... Using Pagemaker 3.0 on the IBM-compatible AT	Balfe	0 434 91318 9	£15.95	....
.... Using Ventura 2.0	Campbell	0 434 90272 1	£15.95	....
.... Wordcraft 6 Handbook	Horrocks	0 434 91324 3	£27.50	....
.... Wordstar Professional Handbook Version 4	Campbell	0 434 90242 X	£19.95	....
.... Programming in GW-Basic	McBride	0 434 91296 4	£14.95	....
.... The PC User's Companion	Sinclair	0 434 91854 7	£16.95	....
.... The Amstrad PC1512/1640 Advanced User's Guide	Reid	0 434 91998 5	£30.00	....
.... The Amstrad PC1512/1640 Owner's Handbook 2nd Edition	Morris	0 434 91376 6	£14.95	....
.... The Software Factory	Johnson	0 7506 0145 0	£40.00	....
.... Computer Security Solutions	Hruska	0 632 02696 0	£35.00	....
.... Database Management Systems	Gorman	0 7506 0135 3	£40.00	....
.... Secure Information Transfer	Jackson	0 632 02664 2	£29.95	....
.... The Scanner Handbook	Beale	0 434 90069 9	£19.95	....
.... Fax User's Guide	Fishman	0 434 90602 6	£10.95	....
TEXTBOOKS				
.... Computer Science	Sinclair	0 7506 0252 X	10.95	....
.... Information Technology Applications	West	0 434 92237 4	£7.95	....
.... Students' Guide to Desktop Publishing	Sinclair	0 7506 0074 8	£9.95	....
.... Student's Guide to Business Computing	Blewett	0 434 91877 6	£9.95	....
.... Student's Guide to Data Communications	Gandoff	0 434 90700 6	£12.95	....
.... Student's Guide to Databases	Bull	0 434 90081 8	£10.95	....
.... Student's Guide to Expert Systems	Marshall	0 434 91306 5	£12.95	....
.... Student's Guide to Information Technology	Carter	0 434 90222 5	£9.95	....
.... Student's Guide to Office Automation	Carter	0 434 90226 8	£9.95	....
.... Student's Guide to Spreadsheets	Sinclair	0 434 91888 1	£9.95	....

☐ Please send me your complete **Computing and Technical Catalogue**	TOTAL THIS PAGE	
	POST AND PACKING	£2.00
	GRAND TOTAL	

☐ I enclose sterling cheque (made payable to RBS Ltd) for £_____

☐ Please debit my ☐ VISA ☐ ACCESS Credit card

Card No_____

Name_____

Address_____

_____

_____

Signature_____ Date_____

Please return this form to: Martin de la Bedoyère, Butterworth-Heinemann, Linacre House, Jordan Hill, Oxford. OX2 8DP   BHBBFUT991